RAMBLI WAKEFIELD

42 MOSTLY CIRCULAR WALKS WITH SKETCH MAPS

Compiled by

Douglas Cossar

for the Ramblers' Association (West Riding Area)

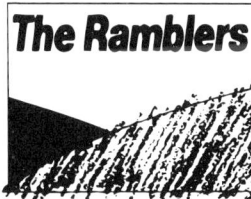

The Ramblers

Other publications by the Ramblers' Association (West Riding Area)

Washburn Valley map & guide
Family Rambles around Bradford
Dales Way Handbook (with the Dales Way Association, annually)
Kiddiwalks (new edition Spring 1995)
Douglas Cossar, *Ramblers' Leeds* (1995)
Douglas Cossar, *The Airedale Way* (1996)

Ramblers' Wakefield first published 1997

© Douglas Cossar 1997

RAMBLERS' ASSOCIATION (WEST RIDING AREA)
27 Cookridge Avenue, Leeds LS16 7NA

ISBN 0 900613 96 3

Cover photographs
Front: Chantry Bridge and Chapel with River Calder, Wakefield
(Ruth Nettleton);
Back: Newmillerdam (Ruth Nettleton), Barbara Hepworth,
The Family of Man in the Yorkshire Sculpture Park (Clare Lilley).

Publishers' Note
At the time of publication all footpaths used in these walks were
designated as public rights of way or permissive footpaths, or were paths
over which access has traditionally not been denied, but it should be
borne in mind that diversion orders may be made or permissions
removed. Although every care has been taken in the preparation of this
guide, neither the author nor the publisher can accept responsibility for
those who stray from the routes described.

Contents

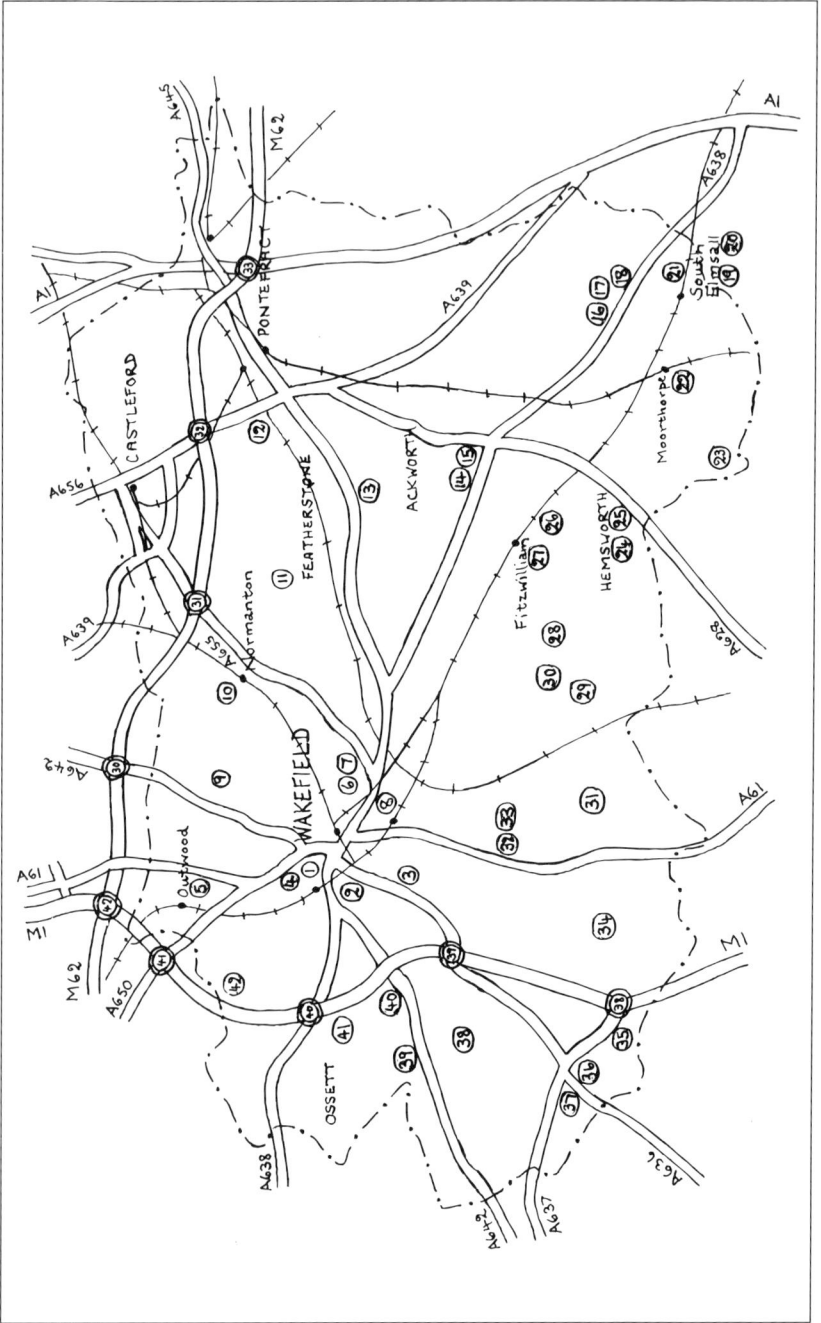

Author's note.

Wakefield in the context of this book means the Metropolitan District of Wakefield, which covers some 130 square miles and has a population of 317,000. In addition to Wakefield City there are five towns in the north east of the District, Castleford, Featherstone, Knottingley, Normanton and Pontefract, the towns of Ossett and Horbury in the north west and the smaller settlements of Hemsworth, South Elmsall and South Kirkby in the south east. There are also numerous villages of various sizes, Ackworth being the largest. Surrounding and separating these towns and villages the landscape is a mixture of farmland (which covers just over half the total land area), woodland, lakes, inland waterways, commons, country parks, large estates such as Bretton Hall, Woolley Hall and Nostell Priory, reclaimed and derelict land. Whilst the landscape would not be described as dramatic or being of outstanding natural beauty, it is mainly a pleasant area for countryside recreation.

There are some 325 miles (529 kilometres) of public rights of way giving access into this countryside, together with recognised permissive routes, paths within country parks and mine reclamation areas and paths which have been used by the public over many years but which have no legal status. The rambles in this book try to introduce walkers to the variety of footpaths and landscapes to be encountered in the whole of the Wakefield District. A substantial part of the route of each walk is within the Wakefield District, although I have allowed myself to stray over the border from time to time for the sake of a more interesting ramble. I hope that on the whole the book represents reasonably well the variety and interest of the landscapes of the Wakefield District. Those who live in it have much to be grateful for.

Public paths are on the whole in much better shape now than they used to be, thanks both to the vigilance and pressure of the Ramblers' Association and the Wakefield Footpaths Group and to the committed attitude of Wakefield Countryside Service. If you should encounter any obstacles, obstructions, nuisances or other difficulties, please report them to the Chief Regeneration Officer, PO Box 47, Newton Bar, Wakefield WF1 2YN. Do look out for the occasional bull at large in pastures in the summer months, and take suitable evasive action, even if this means a minor trespass. Better safe than sorry! Frisky young cattle and horses may give you unwelcome attention, particularly if you have a dog, but are rarely dangerous.

Writing a book of walks in a populous and varied Metropolitan District has taught me how much our environment is constantly changing, and our footpaths with it. New houses and housing estates are built, new roads appear and old ones are widened and upgraded, old coal mines are landscaped and become country parks, the course of canals and rivers is changed, not to mention the wear and tear on stiles and gates, fences and walls; and of course footpaths can be closed or diverted and new ones created. I hope that my descriptions are reasonably up to date, although I am aware that as a result of road-building projects soon to be carried out some of them may not be accurate for very long, and I am most grateful to officers of the Wakefield Countryside Service for reading the manuscript and for suggesting corrections and improvements. The final responsibility for the walks is of course my own.

All the walks can be located on the Ordnance Survey Landranger maps 104 (Leeds, Bradford & Harrogate), 105 (York), 110 (Sheffield & Huddersfield) and 111 (Sheffield & Doncaster), and at the start of each walk I have given details of the relevant Pathfinder sheet(s). The sketch maps which accompany each walk are based on these Pathfinder maps and are reproduced with the permission of the Controller of H.M.S.O. © Crown copyright (43323U). They are intended to give an overview of the walk and to supplement the description, but as they are greatly simplified, particularly in built-up areas, **they should not be used as a substitute for the description.** Please read the descriptions carefully: I have tried to make them clear and unambiguous and to eliminate the risk of misinterpretation. I am sure you will let me know where I have failed! But in my experience lots of people go astray through not concentrating on the text of a walk, inadvertently skipping a line or jumping by mistake from one stile to the next, or just losing the place through being engrossed in conversation with their companions!

All the walks are accessible by public transport, and I have given details as they are known to me at the moment. But please do check this information with the West Riding Automobile Co Ltd for buses (Tel: 01924-360000) or West Yorkshire Metro for trains (Tel: 0113-245-7676).

I am grateful to all who have helped in the production of this book, especially Ruth Nettleton of the Wakefield Footpaths Group, a society affiliated to the Ramblers' Association, and Ralph Denby, Chairman of the Association's Wakefield Group, who have been involved with the project since its inception and have discussed with me every aspect of its production. Ruth suggested many of the walks in the western half of the District, and I am grateful for the patient way she has put up with my mauling her routes around. Ralph has provided the public transport details, has diligently taken up footpath problems with the Council's officers and has walked many of the routes and sent me detailed comments on them.

Douglas Cossar
April 1997

WAKEFIELD CITY TRAIL
WALK 1

No one would claim that Wakefield is one of England's most beautiful cities, and yet a walk around the city centre is still, in spite of extensive demolition and re-development, architecturally and historically rewarding. Among the highlights are the cathedral and the chantry chapel from the Middle Ages, the Elizabethan grammar school, the Georgian brick terraces of St John's Square, St John's North and South Parade, along with Westgate Chapel and the Orangery, and for canal enthusiasts Fall Ings Cut. All these and many more are visited on the recently inaugurated Wakefield City Trail, with an excellent guidebook by Christine Johnstone, on sale at Wakefield Museum, price £2.50, which is supplemented by information boards set up at key points along the route.

Our walk, which starts and finishes at the Wakefield Museum on Wood Street, follows the main city trail (waymarked with red discs with a black arrow) and the southern loop (waymarked with blue discs with a black arrow). Allow at least three hours.

From the Museum walk up Wood Street past the Town Hall and then the Courthouse, built in 1810. Cross Cliff Parade and pass County Hall. On the other side of the road are part of Barbara Hepworth's "Family of Man" sculptures. Turn left along Newstead Road then right along Margaret Street, passing on the right Wakefield Girls' High School. As you reach St John's Square, there is an information board about it. The church was built in 1791-95. Turn right along St John's Square and at the far end cross Wentworth Street and turn left for a look at St John's North, built 1791-96, then return and walk down Wentworth Street, passing Clayton Hospital. Turn left along Wentworth Terrace past Wakefield Art Gallery. There is an information board about the gallery on the railings. Pass on the right St Austin's catholic church and turn right along Northgate. Cross Rishworth Street, pass the Registry Office, built in 1811 as a private house, and a small half-timbered building dating back to Elizabethan times, and at the end of the street cross the crossing to the paved area (information board).

The statue of Queen Victoria was erected in 1905. Walk on in the direction the queen is facing, along the Bull Ring, and turn left into Cross Square (information board). Turn right at the bottom, then left around the cathedral, which dates largely from the 14th and 15th centuries, then go left at the end of the cathedral along Teall Street, cross The Springs and turn left, then right into Brook Street, at the end of which on the left is what is now The Elizabethan Gallery, built just after 1591 as Wakefield's grammar school and one of the most delightful buildings in the town. Cross through the outdoor market and turn right at the far side, then take the second left, which is Zetland Street. Pass on the left the Masonic Hall and on the right the old vicarage, now the Conservative Club.

At the end turn right down Vicarage Street, and at its end go left into Warrengate. Here on the left is an information board. Warrengate is named after the de Warenne family, who came over with William the Conqueror and in about 1106 were made Lords of the Manor of Wakefield. It was they who built Sandal Castle. At the end go through the subway, then right through the car park, on the far side passing round a bollard and down St Clair Street. At the bottom turn left, at the T-junction cross the road and turn right, and when you reach the large roundabout there is an information board. Immediately before the board pass the bollards and walk along John Street. Turn right along Brunswick Street, cross it and turn left along Monk Street. Before you reach Kirkgate Station there is an information board about it on the left.

Now we'll join the southern loop. Turn right on a paved footpath just before the station wall and follow it down to Kirkgate. Turn left and pass under the railway. Take the second road on the left, and a short distance along there is an information board on the left about the Aire & Calder Navigation. Cross the old bridge, built in the 1340s, past the chantry chapel, first built c.1350. At the far end of the bridge turn left over the packhorse bridge built in 1730 and follow the parkland path parallel to the River Calder. Cross Fall Ings Cut by the high footbridge and turn right. There is an information board on the left about the Calder & Hebble Canal, which links Wakefield with Sowerby Bridge. Follow the path along by the canal to a large metal gate, pass round it and keep forward up to the main road.

Turn right along it as far as a traffic island, cross and walk up Sugar Lane with Wakefield Cemetery on the left. Just before you turn right into Welbeck Street there is an information board on the cemetery wall. At the far end of Welbeck Street cross the main road (information board about stagecoaches and toll roads) and turn right along the Barnsley Road towards the city centre. Cross the canal at Fall Ings Basin (information board), cross the Calder by the new bridge first built in 1933 (information board on the far side), then keep forward - there is a very nasty road crossing, with traffic coming fast over the bridge and swinging left - to pass under the railway again, and now we are back on the main city trail.

At the far end of the Magnet building turn left along Charlotte Street, then first right, and left along the cobbled lane (information board where the lane narrows). At the end of the lane cross the road and turn right, then turn left into the old burial ground, which you leave again in the far right hand corner. Turn left for a yard or two, then right up the hill, then left at the top along South Parade, built in the 1790s. Notice the private gardens of the houses on the left. At the far end turn right through the car park, pass through the bollards and turn left. Get across the main road somehow - the bend on the left is blind - and turn right up Market Street, noticing the information board on the corner. Pass an old chapel on the right and another on the left and turn left down Westgate.

On the corner by Unity House there is an information board about the theatre. Cross Westgate to the theatre, turn left and cross Drury Lane, then continue down Westgate. Westgate Chapel, built 1751-52, is set back from the road. Cross the access road to Westgate Station to Pemberton House, built in 1752 for a local cloth merchant. Having passed under the railway bridge, there is an information board on the right about Wakefield Prison. On the corner is Henry Boon's: Henry Boon Clark started brewing in 1905 and opened these premises in 1918. Turn right along Parliament Street. With the prison ahead, turn right up Back Lane, passing once more under the railway. There is an information board on the left about the Orangery, built in the 1760s. At the top of Back Lane on the right is the building which was Wakefield's first public library.

Continue up the hill, crossing the busy road, and turn right along Cheapside. Notice the hoists on the roofs of the former woolstaplers' warehouses, fine old brick buildings built about 1800. Turn left along Westgate. The author George Gissing was born in a house in Thompson's Yard on the left. Turn left through an archway into Barstow Square. Near the top turn right, cross over King Street and walk along Chancery Lane. Turn left at Wood Street and you are back at the Museum. On that last corner there is an information board about it.

THORNES PARK, CANAL AND RIVER
WALK 2

3½ miles (5½ km); Pathfinder 703, 692. Surprisingly "green" for a walk so close to the city centre.

By bus: No. *129 Wakefield-Dewsbury, 443 Leeds-Wakefield-Barnsley, 484 Leeds-Wakefield-Holmfirth to the Holmfield car park.*

By car: Park in the Holmfield car park, below the Holmfield Arms Hotel, on the A636 Wakefield-Denby Dale road.

From the car park, with your back to the main road, turn right towards the old bandstand, a half-timbered building. Pass to the right of it. On the hill to the left is the site of a former castle. Immediately after a fountain on the left turn left, passing another fountain on a climbing path. The grassy area on the right is Clarence Park Arena and in the distance is the city skyline (from right to left the Cathedral, the Town Hall, County Hall and St John's Church). At the next junction ignore a gate on the right out onto the road and pass to the left round the brick gatehouse. Follow the hedge on your right, then walk down the right hand edge of the football/cricket pitch. At the far end turn left along a cross path, with a miniature railway beyond. Pass to the left of the adventure playground.

On reaching the access road to the former Thornes House School, now part of Wakefield College, cross it and turn left up the footway. Leave the buildings of Wakefield Arts Centre and the College on the right, and when the road forks keep left. The road begins to descend, and fenced/hedged in on the left is a miniature golf course. Just after a track comes in from the right fork half right off the road, but keep on parallel to it, walking between the trees and the football pitches, down towards a car park. Bear right round the car park to join a tarmac track. Turn right along it, with the lake to the left. At the end of the lake on the right there is an aviary. Keep forward, and at the end of the rhododendrons on the right there is access on the right to the walled garden and glasshouse. Turn left at the T-junction, with the brick wall ahead, and leave the park.

Turn left, passing the Cathedral School on the other side of the road, and after 60 yards cross the road to follow a paved path down the side of the school grounds. When the paved path ends, keep forward, and follow the school boundary until you reach a lane. Turn right along it, with a new residential development on the left, and soon with Wakefield Municipal Golf Course on the right. The lane turns left and then at the end of the houses curves right and meets a cross track. Turn left to pass under the railway. On the far side of the bridge keep forward up the embankment, then drop to the canal towpath. Turn left along it.

Pass under the A636 to reach Thornes Lock, where the canal rejoins the river, and continue along the riverbank. Far over on the right is Sandal Castle. Pass under the mainline railway, noticing the fine stone bridge abutments, and continue by the river, now in less attractive surroundings, until the path joins a road. Keep forward along it. The large redbrick building you pass on the left is the Double Two shirt factory. Pass The Jolly Sailor and admire the old stone warehouses on the other bank of the river. Opposite the Sea Cadets Headquarters turn left along Thornes Lane. As you pass under the next railway bridge, look left for a fascinating complex of arches, then immediately after the bridge cross the road and walk along Avondale Way.

When the road ends, keep forward to pass under the Wakefield-Huddersfield railway, then continue forward. At the far end cross the dual carriageway by the crossing and turn left, then right up Park Avenue. Take the first entrance into the park on the left and keep left. Follow this path all the way back to your starting point, noticing across the main road on the left St James's Church, built in 1829-31 in the classical style.

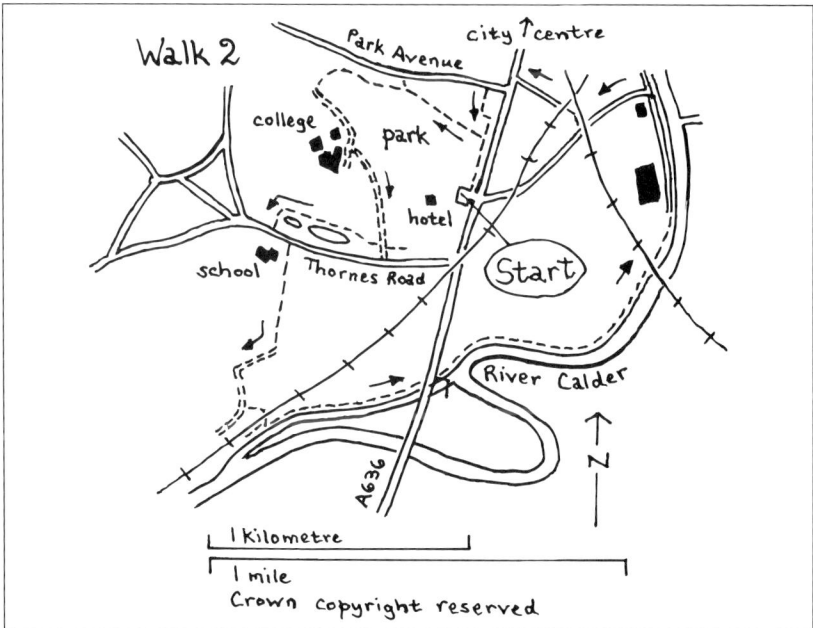

Walk 2

city centre
Park Avenue
college
park
hotel
school
Thornes Road
Start
River Calder
N
A636
1 Kilometre
1 mile
Crown copyright reserved

11

PUGNEYS AND SANDAL CASTLE
WALK 3

4½ miles (7 km); Pathfinder 703; a country park and nature reserve, and a castle ruin with fine views. Pugneys Country Park is run by Wakefield Leisure Services. Canoes, pedaloes, sailing dinghies and windsurfers can be hired, and an electric launch carrying eight people can be hired for a 30 minute trip round the lake.

By bus: The 443 Hall Green/Barnsley bus from Wakefield and the 484 Leeds-Wakefield-Holmfirth bus will drop you near the access road to Pugneys.

By car: Pugneys Country Park is situated on the A636 Wakefield-Denby Dale road. The entrance is from a roundabout, and it is well signposted. There is a large car park.

From the Information Centre or main car park at Pugneys set off walking round the large lake in a clockwise direction on the grass, passing several picnic tables, with Sandal Castle straight ahead in the distance. Gradually bear left onto the surfaced path. Pass through a gap in a metal barrier to reach a broader track, turn left along it for 15 yards, then fork right off it along a path on top of a grassy embankment. A smaller lake is over to your left. Where the embankment begins to bear left, fork right down off it on a path which soon reaches the bank of the River Calder. Bear left along it and follow it to the A636.

Cross straight over and take the track opposite (signposted Calder Grove), but after a few yards pass through a gap by a large gate on the right onto the "Soap Tips". These are the residue from a former soap factory, pollution from which affected among other things trees on Squire Waterton's estate at Walton Hall. The path runs parallel to the track below, past cliffs of residue. Soon you have a fence on your right, with the river down below, but in a short distance you bear left away from it again and cross towards the fence on the left. Where this ends, descend by steps to return to the track and turn right along it. Immediately before Boat House Farm follow the track as it turns left, pass through the gravel extraction works, and when just before Grange Farm you meet a tarmac road, turn left along it and follow it back to the roundabout on the A636. Walk anticlockwise round this and follow the Pugneys access road back to the Information Centre.

This time take the path leading anticlockwise round the large lake. At a fork by a wooden notice board go right to visit the hide in the nature reserve by a smaller lake, then return to this point and continue round the large lake. At the next Nature Reserve notice board fork right off the surfaced track along a grassy track which soon bears right with an overgrown drainage ditch to the left. The track narrows to a footpath and reaches a fork: go left through metal barriers and over the drain, then follow the path to Castle Farm. Turn right along the access road for 15 yards to a stile on the left. Walk up the left hand edge of the field, but when the wall ends cross left into the next field and walk up the right hand edge of this with an old hedge on your right.

When the path forks near the top of the field, go left, to enter Sandal Castle by a redundant stile. At the bench turn right round the perimeter path. There are extensive views to the west, and further round over Wakefield city centre. When a path from the castle car park joins you from the right, look down to where the boundary wall becomes a hedge. Here there is a gap, which is where our walk will continue. But first keep on round to the point where you can fork left up to the old entrance to the castle. Explore the ruins, then return to go through the gap between hedge and wall and immediately turn left along a narrow hedged footpath.

When the hedge on the left turns left, keep straight forward across the field to the houses, cross a cross path and take the tarmac path down the left hand side of them. At the end of the houses keep left and drop to cross another cross path, go over the bridge ahead, pass through a kissing-gate and walk forward to the top of the embankment. Turn left along it. When your way is blocked by a wood, drop down right and follow the edge of the wood to rejoin the surfaced path round the large lake. Turn right along it, shortly forking left, to return to the starting point.

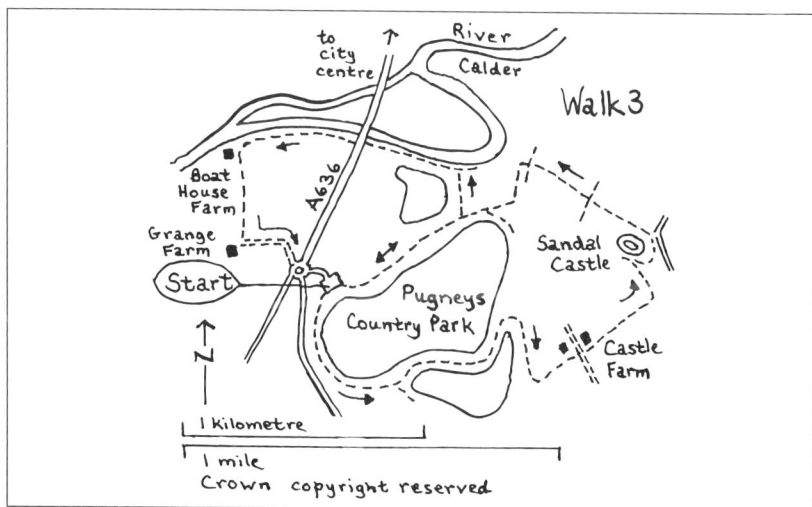

13

ST. JOHN'S SQUARE TO STANLEY MARSH AND STANLEY FERRY
WALK 4

6¼ miles (10 km); Pathfinder 692. A "green" walk from Wakefield city centre to a nature reserve and the canal. Birdwatchers should remember their binoculars. There is a pub halfway round.

By bus: 423/5/6/7 Bradford-Wakefield, 484 Leeds-Wakefield-Holmfirth, 130 Leeds-Wakefield pass St.John's Square.

By car: You cannot park in St.John's Square, but there is free parking in St. John's North at weekends. On weekdays either use public transport or, less satisfactorily, park at the Stanley Marsh Nature Reserve, found by following the A642 Wakefield-Oulton road. At the Grove Park Hotel turn into Lime Pit Lane (signposted to Lee Moor, Lofthouse Gate and Outwood), proceed for 200 yards, pass the renovated property on the left and immediately after it park in the reserve car park. Start the walk at [*] below.

The walk starts at St.John's Square, Wakefield's only bit of Georgian town planning. St.John's Church was built in 1791-5 and extended eastwards in 1905. From the east end of the church cross Wentworth Street and walk along St. John's North, built at the same time as the church. Cross Northgate at the traffic lights and walk down Westfield Road opposite. After 40 yards turn left along a ginnel, with the West Yorkshire Police Headquarters to the right. After a time you enter a hedged path with sports grounds to left and right. The path turns sharp left and in 80 yards sharp right again (ignore the path straight on here), still between hedges. When the hedge on the right ends, keep forward along the left hand edge of the field, and at the end of the houses on the left turn sharp left into another section of hedged path.

In just over 100 yards turn sharp right again (ignoring the path forking slightly left), and when the path ends, turn right to pass to the left of a garage and through a barrier, then bear left, and when you reach the field turn right and walk up its right hand edge with a hedge to your right. In the next field corner you meet a track coming through the gap ahead: turn left along this track. Pass the sad ruins of Stanley Royd Farm and a splendid view over Stanley to the M62 opens up. At the next road turn right for a few yards then go through the kissing-gate by the large double gate on the left. In a few yards you reach a track junction: keep ahead down the left hand track, across Hatfeild Hall golf course.

The track bends right and drops to reach a cross track. Turn right here on the main track, but in 60 yards, where the end of a wall is visible ahead, take the left fork, and follow this track, still through the golf course, until you reach a tarmac drive. Cross it and continue straight ahead, following the path through the wood to a footbridge. Cross this and turn right along a track through the wood. Cross a cross track used by golfers, and a few yards further on fork left on a path which leads to a kissing-gate into StanleyMarsh Nature Reserve. Follow the clear path forward over the field, with the A642 and houses over to the right. A few yards before the path leaves the reserve by another kissing-gate, fork left and climb slightly for a view over the lake, a fine spot for waterfowl, then keep on the path down the slope, there are some broad steps, and a few yards along a wooden boardwalk fork right to reach the reserve car park.

[*] Walk to the car park entrance and turn right along Lime Pit Lane. Cross over the A642 and take the footpath to the right of the farm

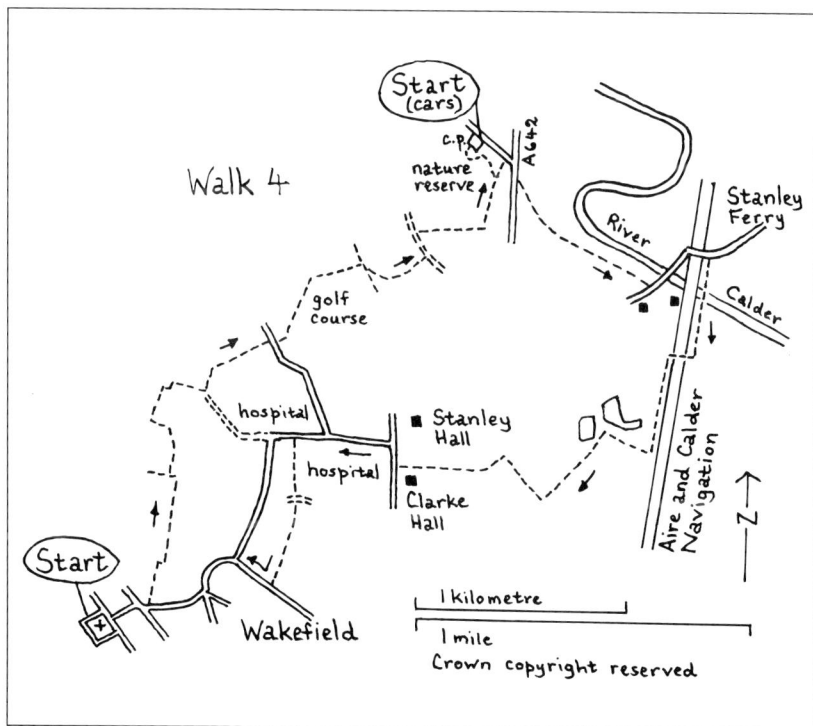

Walk 4

Crown copyright reserved

15

entrance, an old railway line ("The Nagger Line"). Just after a farm on the left keep left at a fork (i.e. straight ahead) on the narrower path and follow it to the next road. The Ship Inn is just to the right and the entrance to the Ferry Boat Inn, which is situated by the canal, immediately opposite. Turn left along the road, cross the River Calder (from the bridge there is a good view of the aqueduct which carries the Aire & Calder Navigation over the River Calder; opened in 1839, this iron construction was the first suspension aqueduct to be built anywhere in the world) and then the canal, and immediately turn right down the steps and walk along beside the canal.

Cross the river by the bridge and continue by the canal as far as the next footbridge over it, Ramsdens Bridge. Cross this (visitors to the Ferry Boat Inn can reach this point directly along the towpath) and continue along the towpath. After 500 yards, just after a bench and just before a British Waterways sign for Stanley Ferry Visitor Moorings, turn right off the towpath through a metal barrier, in a few yards crossing a plank bridge. Pass a pylon (ignore a left fork here) - the lake is a good place for waterfowl - and follow the clear path to another metal barrier. Turn right along the track over a plank bridge, then turn left at the T-junction, with another lake on the right.

Soon a fenced path leads towards houses. Follow it round the outside of the estate. Where it bears left there is a good view right to Stanley Hall, the large white house, now Wakefield Hospice. When the hedged path opens out and forks, with a wood ahead, keep left and walk along for a view of the 16-17th-century Clarke Hall, which groups of schoolchildren visit to experience life as it was lived in olden days. With the Hall ahead turn right along the edge of the wood, then left along a path with a hedge to the right and outbuildings of the Hall to the left. Cross the main road (there is a crossing) and turn right past an entrance to Pinderfields Hospital. Turn left along Bar Lane.

Ignore Ouchthorpe Lane on the right and keep forward along the broad grass verge. After 160 yards, at the end of the hospital boundary wall on the left, turn left along a paved footpath between hedges. This is Long Causeway, which passes through the old Pinders Fields. Cross over a cross path, and now you have a high wall to the left. The path drops, passes a terrace of houses and reaches Eastmoor Road. Turn right along it, passing Wakefield Sports Club, and keep on the main road as it turns left. Turn right up Westfield Road, passing on the left six almshouses built in 1887. At the top you have rejoined your outward route. Cross over Northgate and walk along St. John's North to return to St. John's Square.

OUTWOOD AND WRENTHORPE
WALK 5

6½ miles (10½ km); Pathfinder 692. An exploration of the countryside north and north-east of Wakefield city centre.

By train: _The walk starts at Outwood Station._

By car: _Car park at Outwood Station._

From the car park cross the railway by the road bridge and turn down the steps on the left. Bear slightly right and pass through the stile between two gates, then after 40 yards turn right down some steps, up some more and keep forward. You are joined by a path coming in from the right. Drop to cross a beck by a footbridge and immediately fork right, soon entering a path with a fence and a disused railway on the right. The path joins a track which you follow to the next road. Cross the road and turn left, and take the fenced ginnel on the right after the bungalow number 75A. At a junction ignore the path turning left and keep forward along the fenced path which soon turns left and passes to the left of a small children's playground and the Woodman pub. At the end cross a footbridge on the left and climb steps to the A61.

Cross the road and turn right for a few yards to find steps on the left leading back down to the trackbed of the former railway. Follow this along, crossing over a street, and on reaching the next road, cross diagonally left to the continuation of the footpath. Ignore an unofficial path forking left over the grass and take the descending path. A yard or two before a large pylon just to the left of the path fork right through the bushes along a path which soon becomes tarmac and follow it in a straight line all the way to the next main road (Rook's Nest Road). Turn right for about 400 yards then take the signposted path on the left, which soon passes to the left of farm buildings and joins a track.

Ignore a track forking right and a path forking left, after which your track narrows to a footpath: follow it until it crosses a footbridge and you are faced by a stile onto Hatfeild Hall golf course. Ignore this and turn right along a path with the golf course on your left. Ignore a path forking left to a disused tip. After passing the tip the path becomes fenced and leads up to a road (Ouchthorpe Lane). Turn left for about 250 yards, then just before a high metal fence turn right through a barrier. The path turns left with the fence, then bears right away from it, along the right hand edge of a wood, then through trees, and eventually bears left into a field. Follow the right hand edge of the field to the far end, then keep forward again through trees with a fence on the right.

Pass to the left of an open grassy area and continue forward to the next corner, where a path comes in from the left, following a fence down the field. Keep forward with this hedge to your left on a path which soon bends right to reach a street through a barrier. Ignore the continuation of the path on the left and walk down the street to the A61. Cross diagonally left to the signposted bridleway opposite along a track. Cross over the A650 dual carriageway and take the track opposite. It passes the interesting Red Hall (planned developments here may change the line of the right of way: look out for waymarks) and leads to the old Bradford Road. Cross this and walk down Wrenthorpe Road opposite. Pass under the railway line and in 150 yards take the entrance into the park on the left signposted Cycle Route to City Centre.

The tarmac drive passes to the left of a car park and a football pitch. Cross over a cross path and follow the main path to a footbridge, ignoring a narrower path forking left along to the left of a pond. Having crossed the bridge fork right and then take the right hand of the two paths across the grass towards a hedge on the far side with the tower of Alverthorpe Church in the distance. Pass a redundant stile, cross through the hedge and keep forward with an old hedge on your right towards Silcoates School. When the hedge ends, ignore a track crossing on the right and keep forward to cross a stile into the trees. The hedged path soon turns right and then left again and leads through the school grounds. Look back for a view to the city centre. Pass to the left of the

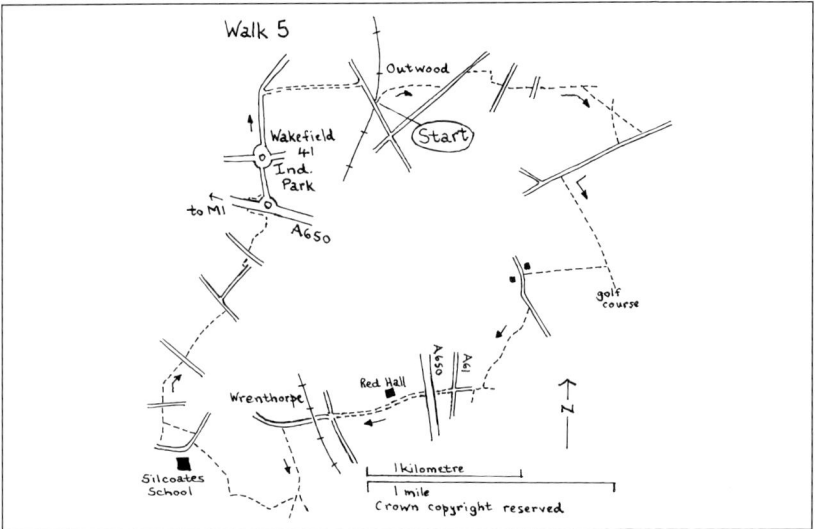

Walk 5

Outwood

Start

Wakefield 41 Ind. Park

to M1

A650

golf course

Red Hall

Wrenthorpe

A650 A61

N

Silcoates School

1 kilometre
1 mile
Crown copyright reserved

18

school car park, and where the road bends left, keep forward along the continuation of the fenced path.

Cross the next road and turn right, pass the end of Silcoates Drive and after house number 40 turn left along a ginnel. Follow this to a T-junction with another paved path and turn right along it. Cross the next road diagonally right to the continuation of the ginnel, which drops steeply to the next street. Cross this and continue down the ginnel opposite. Cross a footbridge and keep on along the fenced path, passing to the left of Jerry Clay Lane School. At Jerry Clay Lane turn right for 20 yards then take the enclosed path to the right of a track on the left and follow it to the next road, crossing a footbridge in the dip. Turn left, then right along Cricketers Approach.

Follow the street almost to the end, then turn left before the last house to find an enclosed footpath which leads to the next road. Cross it and turn left for 50 yards to a track on the right. When this turns right to a house, keep forward up the slope, soon with a high fence on the left. Follow this up to the top and down the other side, and walk forward almost to the dual carriageway, there turning left along a footpath. Shortly this bears right up to the main road. Cross and turn right along the footpath on the other side, then left at the roundabout into the Wakefield 41 Industrial Park. Keep straight on at the next roundabout, then a short distance before the road begins to curve right take the track on the right which has a brick wall to its left. This leads to Lingwell Gate Lane, and Outwood Station is a few yards along to the right.

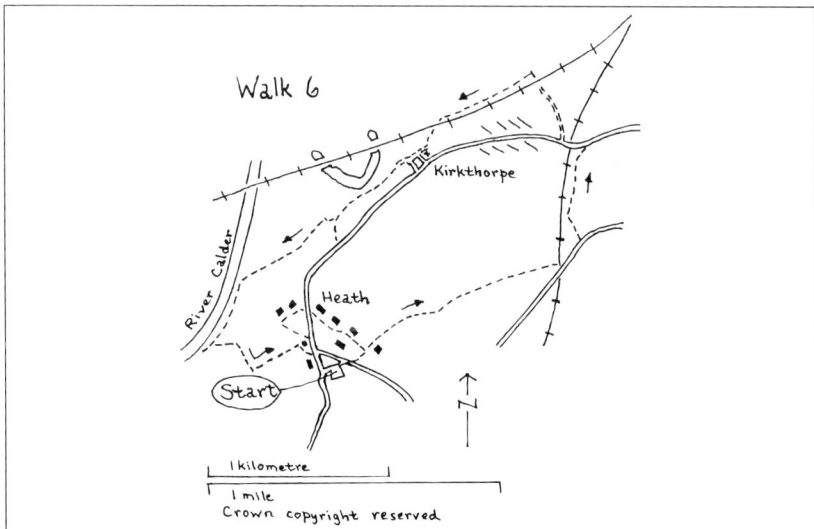

Walk 6

Kirkthorpe

River Calder

Heath

Start

1 kilometre

1 mile

Crown copyright reserved

19

HEATH AND KIRKTHORPE
WALK 6

4¼ miles (6¾ km); Pathfinder 692, 703; an exploration of two of Wakefield's architecturally most rewarding villages, linked by pleasant countryside.

By bus: No. 172, 182, 192, Wakefield-Pontefract bus to Heath.

By car: park in the main car park at Heath.

Leave the car park by the main entrance and walk straight across the grass, cross the first tarmac road and head for the bus shelter. Pass it and continue along the footway, and after the next house on the left walk diagonally left over the grass towards a large mansion at the far end. To the left of this notice the elaborate gateposts of the 16th-century Heath Old Hall, demolished in the early sixties. Adjacent is the priest's house. Progress round the edge of the green in a clockwise direction, passing the large mansion, which is Heath House, designed by James Paine (who was responsible for Nostell Priory) and begun in 1744. A little further on is the magnificent Heath Hall, with its matching buildings at either side, designed by John Carr for the Smyth family in 1753. Bear right past the front of the Hall to the Dower House, another 18th-century mansion.

Follow the curve of the green to the left. The house straight ahead of you is the 17th-century Marsh Close, which previously had a thatched roof, and shortly after is the 16th-century Old School House. The next large mansion is the 18th-century Beech Lawn. Walk along the edge of its ha-ha, and straight ahead of you is the 18th-century Manor House, formerly a residence of the Bishops of Wakefield, now a nursing home. Bear left before you reach it to a stile in the wall, and walk up the hedged path. At the end go through the kissing-gate on the right and bear half left over the field to another kissing-gate where the fence joins the hedge on the far side. The mound on your left is Mount-Tarry-by-it, on which there was at one time a summerhouse belonging to the Hall, which gave an overal view of Heath.

Bear left with the wall on your left. About 120 yards from the end of the field, where there should be a waymark post, bear at an angle of about 25° across the field to a gap in the hedge marked by another post. Continue in the same direction over the next large field to the road and turn left along the footway. Cross the old railway bridge and pass the mushroom farm, then immediately turn left along the track signposted public bridleway. The path soon enters an old hedged way. Turn left at the next road, but just after crossing the old railway again (here looking more like a canal!), turn right along the signposted track. Cross the level crossing with care and turn left along the path beside the railway.

Having passed through a metal barrier you soon pass under the railway. On the far side bear right up the tarmac lane to Kirkthorpe. On reaching the houses the lane turns left, then right, and passes to the right of the church. This is a delightful secluded spot.

Enter the churchyard by steps near the road junction and walk past the main door to the east end. The gravestones with large incised crosses commemorate nine Benedictine nuns who escaped the French Revolution in 1792 and lived at Heath Hall between 1811-21. Leave the churchyard by the main gate and turn right, passing the end of Half Moon Lane. On the right are the village stocks. Behind them and to the left are Frieston's Hospital Almshouses. Turn back and walk down Half Moon Lane. Notice the old Cheesecake Inn on the right, dated 1740. On the left is the back view of the hospital, where a plaque informs us that it was founded in 1595 by John Frieston of Altofts. Below it is the old schoolhouse, built in 1899.

Turn left at the next junction, along an unsurfaced track which soon narrows to a footpath. After a short distance you can either stay on the higher path or go down steps on the right for a closer look at Half Moon Pond, on the former course of the River Calder and popular with anglers. This lower variant rejoins the main path further on. When the path forks by a large tree at the corner of a field, keep right and follow the fence on the left down into the wood. The path soon bends right along an embankment, (works proposed here may affect access for a time) but after 35 yards drop down left off this and follow a clear path through young woodland all the way to the power station. Immediately before the gate turn sharp left.

The path passes to the right of the Dame Mary Bolles water tower, built about 1650 to provide piped water by gravity feed to her mansion of Heath Old Hall; it was repaired in 1986. The path passes between a field on the left and the power station on the right. When the fence posts on the left end, turn sharp left and follow the path back to the village. Walk forward along the track, which bends right to join a tarmac lane, keep right at the fork and follow the lane along. The first building on the left is the 18th-century Cobblers Hall, then comes the Old Smithy, but before you reach Heath village school, built to replace the old school, bear left over the green. At the motor road the Kings Arms Inn, with its paved floors and gaslight, is straight ahead. The bus shelter is on the left, or bear right over the grass to return to the car park.

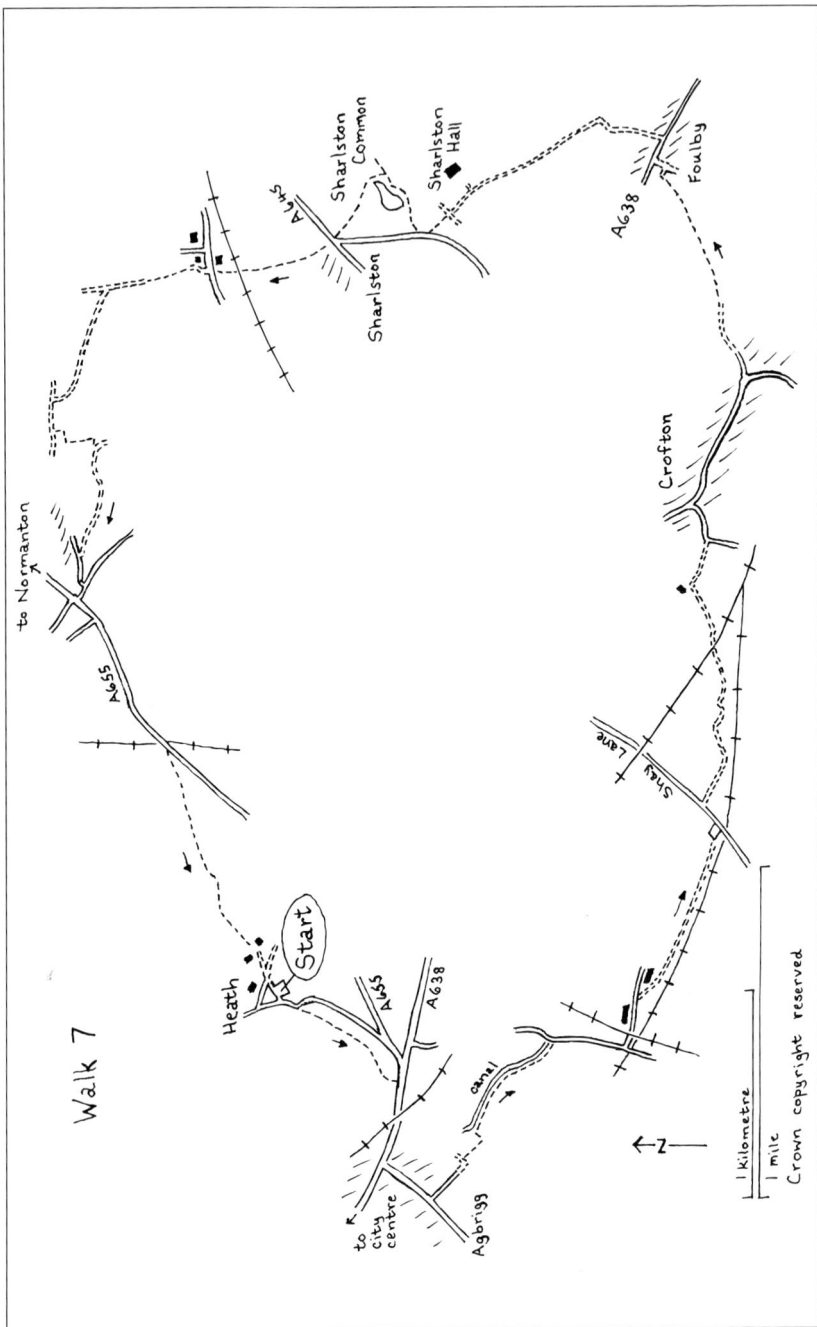

Walk 7

Heath

Start

to Normanton

to city centre

Agbrigg

A655

A638

A638

A655

canal

Shay Lane

Crofton

A638

Foulby

Sharlston Common

Sharlston Hall

Sharlston

A645

←N—

1 kilometre

1 mile

Crown copyright reserved

HEATH TO CROFTON, SHARLSTON AND WARMFIELD
WALK 7

9½ miles (15½ km); Pathfinder 692, 703; an attractive rural circuit, using easy tracks and field paths, and incorporating a delightful stretch of the Barnsley Canal.

By bus: No. 172, 182, 192, Wakefield-Pontefract bus to Heath.

By car: park in the main car park at Heath.

Leave the car park in Heath and turn left, cross over the next road and turn left along the verge, but in a few yards a footpath develops, which descends the right hand edge of the common. About 150 yards down, look left for what seem to be the remains of an old spring. Follow the path all the way to the A638 and turn right along the footway. Pass under the railway bridge, and at the next traffic lights cross the main road and walk along Agbrigg Road. Follow it for 300 yards then turn left along Montague Street. When the houses end, the road leads past allotments, and when the high fence on the left turns left, follow it, but immediately cross to the right and pass between two concrete gateposts to walk along a grassy track with a beck to the right. There are more allotments over to the left behind a high wire fence. When this fence turns left, follow it into an enclosed footpath which leads to the disused Barnsley Canal.

When you reach the towpath, notice the ingenious gate on the left, leading to a section of towpath which is a dead end, and turn right through the metal barrier. There now follows a delightful stretch of towpath, by the canal which is now used by the Walton Angling Club. At the next motor road turn right. Along here there's a pleasant view back to the Wakefield skyline. Just before the road crosses the main railway line turn left along Chevet Terrace, which passes through a tunnel under another railway line. Pass the terrace of brick houses and continue down the road as far as a barrier by a large gate on the right leading to a grit track. The track, which is parallel to the main railway line, leads eventually to another barrier and a large car park on Shay Lane. Leave the car park, cross the road and turn left along the footway.

In about 30 yards turn right along a hedged grassy track and follow this delightful, obviously old path, to a pedestrian crossing over a railway, from where the hedged track continues. On reaching a farmyard turn sharp right, and at the next road turn left over an old brick railway bridge (the railway has disappeared; there is a nice view to the centre of Wakefield from here) and follow the road up to Crofton, passing an old chapel built in 1866 and now a private residence. When you reach the main road cross it and turn right along the footway. You pass the Lord of the Manor pub, an old building of character once lived in by Titus Salt, the founder of Saltaire. Just before the Slipper pub fork left down Spring Lane, and at the end of the street keep on down the track, with a hedge to the left and a new housing estate on the right. Ignore a footpath forking off left and follow the track past old allotments. When you reach a T-junction on the outskirts of Foulby, bear right, and in a few yards at another junction left to reach the A638.

Cross this busy road with care and turn right along it as far as a tarmac lane on the left signposted public footpath. When the tarmac surface ends, keep forward along the track. On approaching Sharlston Hall notice the old dovecote in the field on the right. Sharlston Hall is a superb late-mediaeval timber-framed house with later additions. Keep straight forward down the access road, but where this turns left, keep straight on, crossing another tarmac lane, then over the grass towards a bench and a hedge corner.

Now we shall make a detour over Sharlston Common. Turn right along the road for a few yards, then right again off it along a track. Walk along the right hand edge of a car park and on along the track, soon reaching a lake. Keep forward along the right hand side of this, until the track bears right away from it and you reach a junction. Turn left down to the dam, cross it and keep forward until you reach a junction of paths, where you again keep straight forward, toward the trees. Take the first narrow path forking left, and after a few yards you will see ahead of you in the distance a long terrace of houses. Head towards the right hand end of this, and when you reach a very clear cross track cross straight over. After a time you are walking quite close to the edge of the Common, then just before you reach the road the path bears slightly left and you reach a road junction by a bench.

Cross the main road and pass between the houses opposite to reach a tarmac footpath along the edge of a field. Follow this path to the railway, cross with care, and walk forward along the track to the next road, with the Station Hotel on the right. Cross straight over and take the unsurfaced track opposite. Just after the last house on the right keep left at a fork along a narrow but clear footpath, passing under two sets of power lines, with old mine workings over the fence on the left. Soon a stile leads into a field. Bear slightly left over it to the next stile, then straight over the next one to another stile which gives access to a stony fenced track. Follow this as far as a fork and keep left. The track rises towards a large pylon and passes through a fence. Turn left along the cross track which leads back through the fence when you are level with the pylon. Leave the track here and go through the small gate straight ahead which leads into a fenced footpath.

The path turns right and then left, and now there is only a fence on the left. Soon after it turns right again you lose this fence too and reach a path junction; keep right along a track. Follow this until you reach a narrow road by some houses; bear left along it to a T-junction. Cross the road to the footway and turn right for a few yards to find a footpath forking left up to an old school on the A655. Keep forward along the footway. The Pineapple (John Smith) is reached in a few yards. Cross the road and turn left along the footway on the other side. Pass the mushroom farm and cross a disused railway line, then immediately pass through the old gateway on the right and follow the footpath diagonally left across this very large field.

On the far side of the field cross the little footbridge and go through the gap in the hedge, then continue your line until you meet the wall on the right. Follow it along to a kissing-gate on the right, go through and, facing across the field towards the hedge on the far side, go half left to pass through another kissing-gate in this hedge, which leads into a hedged path. Follow this down to Heath village. Bear right along the tarmac road and keep straight forward at the crossroads to return to the car park.

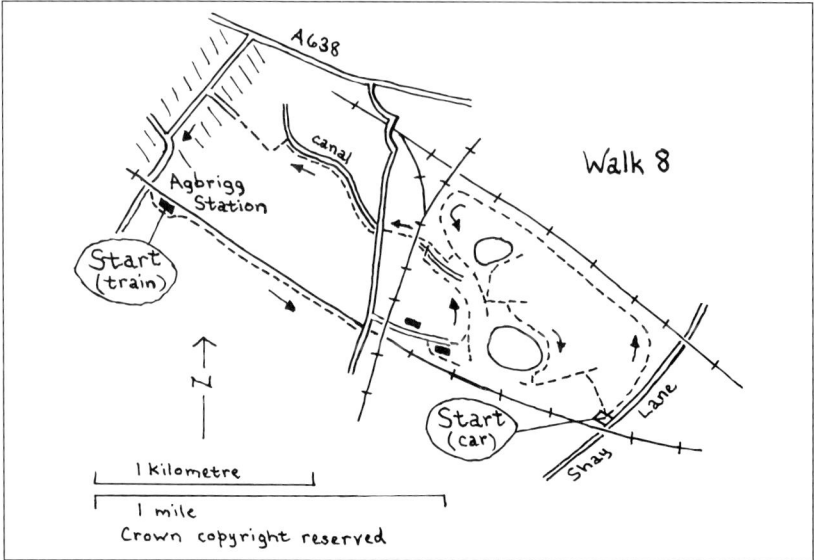

Walk 8

Crown copyright reserved

25

WALTON COLLIERY AND THE BARNSLEY CANAL
WALK 8

4¾ miles (7½ km); Pathfinder 703. Largely an exploration of the reclaimed site of the former Walton Colliery, which has been landscaped with several lakes, which will be of interest to bird watchers. The tracks can be very muddy after a wet spell.

By train: Start at Sandal & Agbrigg Station (Wakefield Line). If arriving from Wakefield, walk down to Agbrigg Road and turn left to pass under the railway bridge, then turn first left again and walk to the far end of the station car park, to start the route description at [#].

By car: Park in the car park on Shay Lane just north of the main line railway (GR 363 175).

Walk towards the car park exit, but just before it turn left over a stone bridge and pass through a barrier, then follow the track with a fence on your right, parallel to the road. When the track curves left, ignore a track forking right off it to a metal kissing-gate. Ignore the next track forking left, and now the first of the lakes is a short distance off to the left. Having crossed another stone bridge, immediately keep right at the fork. There is a railway line up on an embankment to your right. Eventually the track curves left, with another railway high on an embankment ahead. Having crossed a sleeper bridge you reach a crossing of tracks: turn right here, in a few yards crossing a stoutly built wooden bridge, after which the path curves right. To your left is the old Barnsley Canal.

Ignore a bridge on the left crossing the canal and follow the path forward to pass under a very high railway bridge to reach a car park and a road. Cross straight over into a fenced path which follows the canal towpath. When the canal ends, pass through a barrier and turn left down a grassy track with a high fence on the right. The path soon turns sharp right and now follows a beck on the left. On reaching a road, turn left for a few yards, then right, and follow this street to its end at a main road (Agbrigg Road). Turn left along it. Pass under the railway line at Sandal & Agbrigg Station and immediately turn left to walk past the station and through the car park to the far end.

[#] Pass through the gate and keep ahead along the track, which is on the embankment of an old railway (this is the Sandal Curves Railside Footpath). When the path ends at an old railway bridge, drop down some steps on the right to a road. Turn left to pass under the railway bridge. Cross the main line railway and turn right along Chevet Terrace. Follow this road to its end, passing two terraces of houses, one on the left, the other on the right, and pass through the barrier back into the reclaimed site of Walton Colliery.

When you reach a cross track, with a lake over to the right, turn left, soon with the old Barnsley Canal on your right. Follow the path to its end and cross the canal by the bridge. Turn right, back along the other side, until the path bears left over another footbridge and you reach a crossing of tracks. Turn right here. Shortly after crossing a stone bridge you reach another crossing. Bird watchers will want to make the detour to the left, along a track which skirts another lake, but our route takes the track half left. In about 60 yards cross a stile in the fence on the right and follow the track round another lake to another stile. Cross this and turn left. On reaching a fork, turn right to drop to the car park. Train walkers should now return to the start of the walk description.

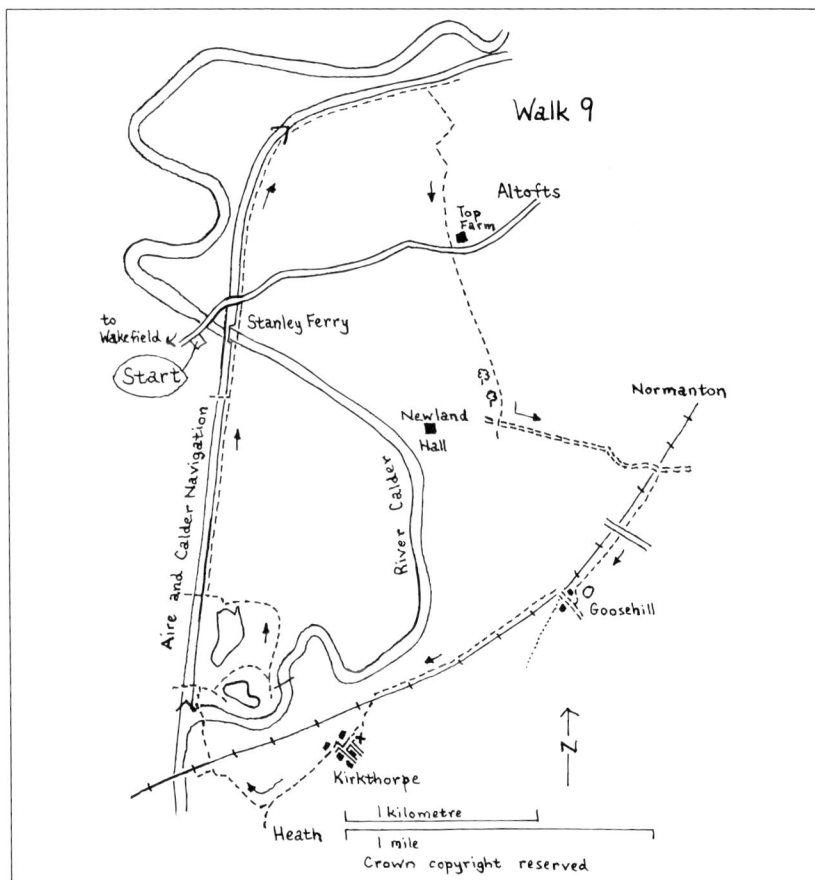

Walk 9

Altofts
Top Farm

to Wakefield
Stanley Ferry

Start

Normanton

Aire and Calder Navigation

Newland Hall

River Calder

Goosehill

Kirkthorpe

Heath

N↑

1 kilometre

1 mile

Crown copyright reserved

STANLEY FERRY TO ALTOFTS AND KIRKTHORPE
WALK 9

6¾ miles (10½ km); Pathfinder 692. A surprisingly rural ramble, with a long stretch of canal towpath and a nature reserve (waterfowl).

By bus: No. 147 Wakefield-Pontefract bus to Stanley Ferry.

By car: park in the car park at Stanley Ferry Marina.

Leave the car park and turn right along the road. Cross the Calder - from the bridge there is a good view right to the arched suspension aqueduct which carries the canal over the river - and having crossed the canal descend the steps on the right and turn right to pass under the road bridge. There follows a quiet rural stretch of towpath. Pass Birkwood Lock, after which the towpath is a tarmac road. Follow this road for about 600 yards, until you reach a stile in the fence on the right (it is a few yards before a slight widening of the road to form a passing place, and where a hedge on the right joins the fence by the canal).

Cross the stile and walk up the edge of the field with the hedge on your left. Go through the gate in the next field corner and keep on with the fence/hedge to your left. In the next corner turn right with the field edge and follow it as far as the next gate on the left. Go through this and walk up the right hand edge of the next field. Go through the gate in the next corner and follow the track diagonally over the next field. In the top corner ignore the track going through a gate on the left and go through the gate in the hedge ahead. Turn left and follow the field edge past Top Farm to a stile in the next corner. Cross straight over the road (Altofts is to your left) to the signposted bridleway opposite and follow the right hand edge of the field on a paved path.

At the end of the field go through a gate and continue forward along the old field boundary, passing under power lines. A short avenue of trees leads to the dilapidated boundary wall of Newland Park: keep forward with this wall on your right. Drop down to reach the old access road to Newland Hall (Newland Lane) and turn left along it.

Pass a tall brick chimney and cross the railway, then in a couple of yards turn right along a clear path which soon passes under a huge pylon and runs parallel to the railway which is in a cutting on the right. Cross a mine access road, pass through the barrier opposite and walk along the track. A few yards before a large gate turn left and continue along a clear path. After a time the path bears left round Goosehill Pond, then right uphill to reach the lane at Goosehill. Pass through the entrance gates on the right (once an entrance to Newland Hall), pass Goosehill Cattery and cross the railway. After the first bridge ignore a wooden gate on the left and keep forward over the second bridge, pass through a metal barrier and bear left with the path, with a high metal fence to your right.

Follow this path parallel to the railway, now on your left, passing at one point a level crossing with a path leading up to Warmfield and Kirkthorpe, until having passed through a metal barrier you soon pass under the railway. On the far side bear right up the tarmac lane towards St. Peter's Church, which is in a small settlement separate from the main part of the village of Kirkthorpe. On reaching the houses the lane turns left, then right, and passes to the right of the church. This is a delightful secluded spot. When the track forks, keep right, i.e. straight ahead, at the T-junction turn right, then left again at the next junction, along an unsurfaced track which soon narrows to a footpath.

After a short distance you can either stay on the higher path or go down steps on the right for a closer look at Half Moon Pond, on the former course of the River Calder and popular with anglers. This lower variant rejoins the main path further on. On reaching a fork with a large tree and fence corner ahead, keep right and follow the fence downhill with a wood to your right. The path soon leads away from the fence down into the wood and turns right along the top of an embankment. Follow this until you are level with a tunnel under the railway on the right, then drop steeply down and go through the tunnel. Follow the path to Blue Bridge and cross the River Calder.

From the bridge walk forward until you reach a cross track. Ignore the canal bridge on the left and the track straight ahead and turn right along the track into the Southern Washlands Nature Reserve. When you reach a fork with a lake ahead keep left. At the next T-junction our route goes left, but it is worth going right for a few yards then left to see the spectacular weir on the river, then retracing your steps. At the next fork in the track keep left, but when this track bears right in front of a fence, keep forward with the fence to your right. After a short distance the fence bears away right, but keep straight on and when your way is barred by a fence turn left down to a hide overlooking another lake.

Come back up again and follow the path forward to another track, which you join over a wooden bridge. Turn left along the track. When you reach a fence with a stile in it, cross the stile and bear right down to the towpath of the Aire & Calder Navigation. Follow the towpath to Stanley Ferry, where you recross the Calder. Climb the steps at the next bridge over the canal and turn left over the bridge to return to your starting point.

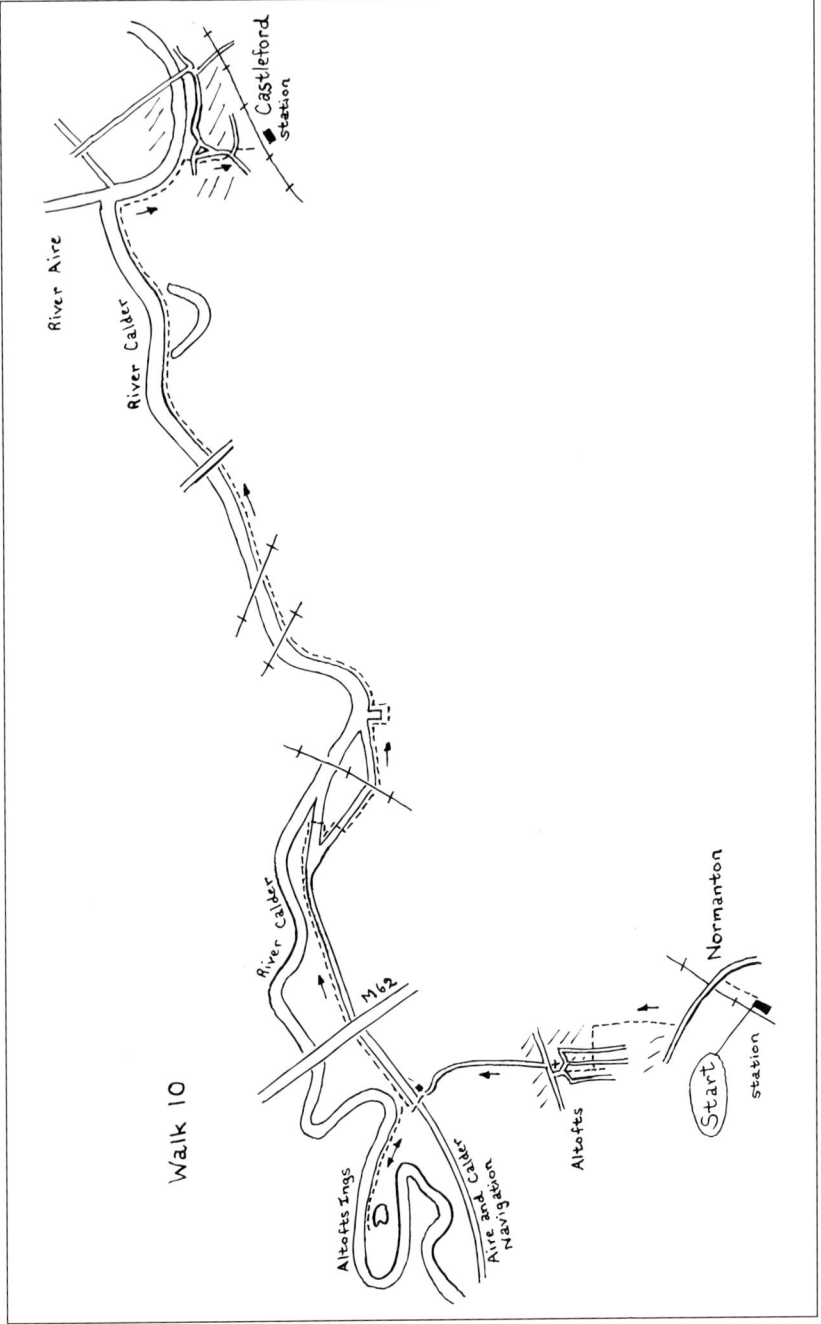

Walk 10

River Aire

River Calder

River Calder

Castleford Station

M62

Normanton

Altofts

Start

station

Altofts Ings

Aire and Calder Navigation

BY CANAL AND RIVER FROM NORMANTON TO CASTLEFORD
WALK 10

7 miles (11 km) LINEAR; Pathfinder 692, 693. An easy, peaceful and pleasant ramble, rural almost all the way, with a detour for birdwatchers to Altofts Ings.

By train: the walk starts at Normanton Station and finishes at Castleford Station (both on the Hallam Line).

By car: park at Normanton Station or in the large car park next to it and return here by train from Castleford.

On leaving Normanton Station turn left and follow the track along the left hand side of the car park and on to the motor road. Turn left over the railway bridge, cross the road and take the first track on the right, which leads to the left of a farm and narrows to a footpath between fields. Just before you reach the next houses turn left along a cross path between hedges. Cross over two streets and when your way ahead is blocked by a fence turn right along another ginnel. At the next street keep forward to pass to the left of the Parish Church of St. Mary Magdalene, Altofts, cross the road ahead and turn right for a few yards then left along Foxholes Lane, which you follow to the Aire & Calder Navigation.

Cross the canal and turn right along the tarmac lane, but immediately before this crosses a bridge with white wooden railings turn left off it to make the short detour to Altofts Ings. Follow the footpath along the bank of the River Calder until you reach a lake on the left. This is a remote and peaceful spot, except for the hum of motorway traffic, popular with birdwatchers. The right of way continues for a short distance further along the river bank, but I suggest you turn here and retrace your steps to the canal.

On reaching the tarmac lane again our way continues left along it, but first you may like to visit the picnic site and information boards just to the left. Follow the "towpath" under the M62 and on to Woodnook Lock, where the canal rejoins the river. Cross the canal by the first lock gate and turn right, to follow the opposite towpath back in the direction you have just come from. But the path soon turns left, then left again along the towpath of an older, now disused stretch of the canal, which you soon cross by a bridge where there was once a lock. Turn left and follow the towpath on the other side of the old cut.

Pass under a railway bridge, and soon you reach the lock where the old cut joined the river: notice the date 1825 on the ironwork. The clear path now leads away from the river, so that you can cross an arm of the canal by a concrete bridge. Turn left again to rejoin the riverbank. The riverside path passes under two railway bridges and a modern road bridge, then through the yard of Methley Bridge Boat Club to a stile/kissing-gate which gives access to the floodbank of the river. Walk along this until your way is barred by a fence: drop left to cross the stile in it, then continue forward through the wooden barrier and on along by the river, now with a high fence on the right.

Pass the confluence of the Calder and the Aire and keep on by the river (now, of course, the Aire!) until your way is blocked by a brick wall. Turn right to the road, cross straight over, pass through the bollards and walk up the street opposite, to pass to the left of Castleford Parish Church. Cross the main road (care!) and immediately after The New Junction pub turn left along Carlton Street, cross it and turn right through arches in the row of shops, then walk forward along the paved way to Castleford Station.

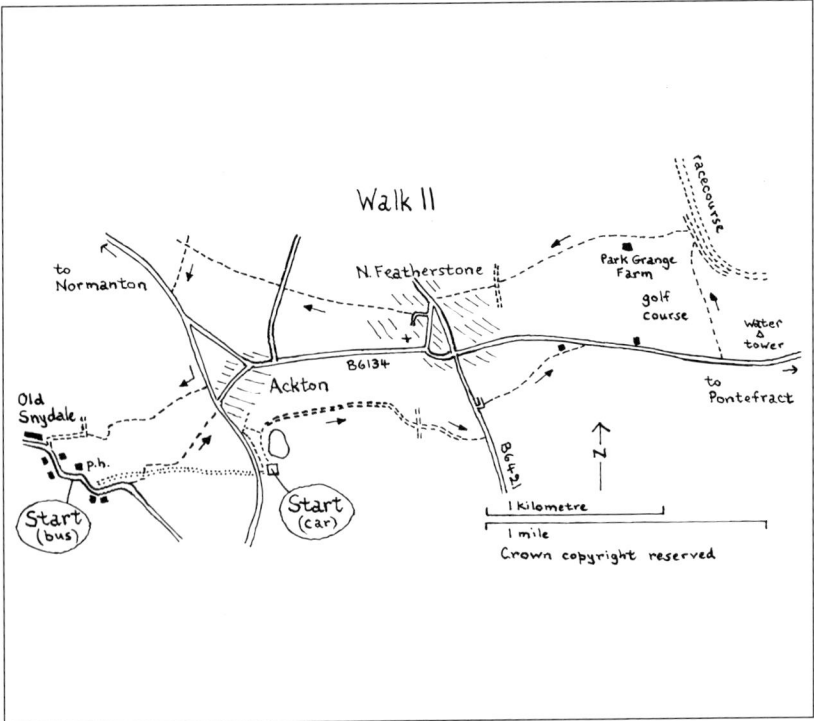

Walk 11

NORTH FEATHERSTONE CIRCULAR
WALK 11

6½ miles (10½ km); Pathfinder 693. The walk traverses the quiet countryside between Pontefract Park and Old Snydale.

By bus: No. 147 Wakefield-Pontefract to the Cross Keys, Old Snydale. The 146/177/178 Pontefract-Castleford and 183 Castleford-South Elmsall could be taken to the junction of Willow Lane and Church Lane in North Featherstone and the walk joined at [*].

By car: Car park at Ackton Pond at the southern end of the Ackton bypass on Sewerbridge Lane (GR 413 213). Walk along to the left of the pond, keeping the fence on your right and ignoring a gate giving access to the pond, and start the walk at [#].

Follow the road past the Cross Keys (on your left). The road bends left and the footway crosses to the other side. Where the road bends right at the end of the 30 mph limit keep straight forward along the footpath which soon turns left and passes through a former tunnel under the railway. Turn right, with the high railway embankment on your right, and soon cross a bridge over Sewerbridge Beck. Walk forward and keep on the left of the field boundary leading away from the railway towards the houses. Soon a track develops, which you follow to the road. Cross and turn right along the footway/verge. At the end of the 30 mph limit go through the metal gate on the left, turn left along the track for two yards then turn right off it to follow a fence on your right to a bridge over a drainage ditch. The walk turns left at this point, but a detour can be made right to visit the Fishermen's Pond (Ackton Pond).(Car walkers will turn right to return to their starting point.)

[#] Follow the track between the ditch on the left and the fence on the right. After a time North Featherstone Church appears on the left on the top of the hill. When you reach a clear cross track, keep forward through the gap by the large metal gate ahead and continue on the track, still with the drainage ditch to your left. Follow the track until on a left hand bend you are faced with padlocked gates and a gap in the fence a few yards to the left of them. Leave the track to go through this gap and immediately turn left along the fence, which you follow to the B6421 (Featherstone Lane).

Cross the road and turn left. Just past a bench turn right along Highfield Close and go through a small gate by a large one at the end, then follow the fence on your left forward. notice the extensive view back, with the Emley Moor mast prominent. Cross a stile and turn left along the left hand edge of a field, then in the next corner turn right with the field boundary. Follow the fence on your left to the B6134, passing a farm with an abundance of free range ducks and chickens, then cross the road and turn right along the footway. Pass the entrance into Pontefract & District Golf Club.

Shortly before you reach the water tower and mound covering an underground reservoir on the left, turn left at a cobbled entrance to a track with a barrier across it. Pass round this, but in a few yards fork left off the track and follow the tall hedge on your left. The path soon acquires a line of tall poplar trees on the right. The grandstand of Pontefract racecourse soon appears over to the right. When the poplars end, keep following the hedge on the left until the path bears right away from it and in a few yards joins a cross track, which runs round the racecourse. Turn left along it, but just before you reach a barrier across it with a stile beside it, turn left and walk along the edge of the golf course with a hedge on your right.

When the hedge ends, keep forward on a clear path which passes some gorse bushes and joins a track which leads to Park Grange Farm. On reaching the farm, keep along the right hand edge of the yard with a hedge on your right, and where this ends at a cross track, keep forward over the next field on a clear path. At the end of the first field cross a plank bridge and continue with a drainage ditch to your left. The path leads in a straight line along the edge of several fields to reach a stile onto the access road to Park Farm. Turn left for a few yards to a stile on the right and follow the path at first with a fence on the right and soon between fences. The path is joined by a ginnel from the left and acquires a tarmac surface. Follow it to the end and keep forward to the junction of Willow Lane and Church Lane in North Featherstone. A short distance to the right is the Bradley Arms.

[*] Cross the main road and bear left down Church Lane. Opposite the post office turn right along Manor Drive, but where this curves left, keep forward along the track. Pass the water tower, squeeze past the barrier over the track and keep forward down the right hand edge of the next field with concrete fence posts on your right. Follow this line to the next road (Ackton is over to your left) cross straight over and follow the clear path forward over the next field, passing under two sets of high power lines and another two sets of lower ones. Go over the footbridge in the next cross hedge and continue over the middle of the next field. Immediately before the next cross hedge turn left along the old Loscoe Lane on a clear path (heading towards a pylon) soon between hedges.

At the road turn left along the footway. Ignore the minor road forking left to Ackton and keep along the footway of the Ackton bypass. About 15 yards before the start of the 30 mph limit cross the road and walk down the tarmac access to a field, cross the stile and follow the left hand edge of the field. Pass under the power lines and cross the stile by the gateway in the next field corner, then follow the left hand edge of the next field. Follow the fence on the left to the next stile, cross it, and in a few yards a plank footbridge, and keep along the left hand edge of the wooded area to a concrete and brick footbridge and stile, then bear left and then right round the edge of the next field. Pass the bollard by the double gate and keep forward along the track into Old Snydale. Cross the road and turn left along the footway to return to the starting point. On reaching the Cross Keys, car walkers will return to the start of the walk description.

PONTEFRACT PARK TO ORCHARD HEAD AND GLASS HOUGHTON
WALK 12

5¾ miles (9¼ km); Pathfinder 693. It is not easy to find pleasant walks between Pontefract and Castleford, but this one is reasonably "green", and of course Pontefract Park is very pleasant.

By train: Start at Pontefract (Tanshelf) station (Metro Pontefract Line). Take the exit into the station car park, which is on the side of trains coming from Wakefield, then walk up the access road and turn right at the T-junction.

By car: The car park in Pontefract Park is reached from a roundabout on the A639 (Park Road) at the south-eastern corner of the park. Walk back up the access road, but instead of turning left to the roundabout, keep straight on past the gateposts to the gate at the far end, turn left and cross the dual carriageway, then turn right for a few yards to take the first street on the left and reach the start of the walk.

Follow the street to the end. It narrows to a tarmac lane. Don't enter the cricket ground but turn left along the path outside its wall. At the far end of the ground turn right again, with a high metal fence on your left, and follow this ginnel to the next road. Turn left, cross the railway by the level crossing, and turn right along Lady Balk Lane, which is the last street on the right before the surfaced road ends.

Follow Lady Balk Lane to the T-junction at the far end, cross the road and turn left for 20 yards to a bridleway on the right between a fence and a hedge. It soon bends left and shortly you have a hedge on the left. Having passed through the remnants of a cross hedge keep left at the fork, follow the hedge up the hill, cross a cross path and take the path opposite, which bears half left and soon drops towards the motorway. Cross a footbridge, pass a pumping station and a stables and turn left along the track parallel to the motorway.

On reaching the road turn right under the motorway bridge and after a further 15 yards cross the road and take the narrow fenced footpath opposite. Keep along the boundary fence of the motorway until the path bears right, crosses a bridge and keeps to the right of a field boundary over the field (about half right from the line of the previous path) At the end of the field turn right with the boundary up the slope. When the field edge turns right again at the top of the slope, keep forward for a few yards to reach a track and turn left along it.

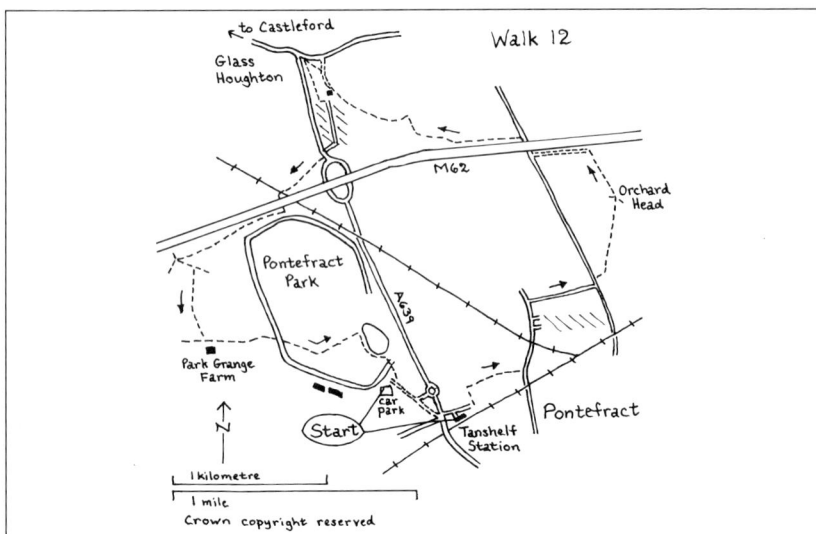

Walk 12

to Castleford
Glass Houghton
M62
Orchard Head
Pontefract Park
A639
Park Grange Farm
Car Park
Start
Tanshelf Station
Pontefract
N
1 kilometre
1 mile
Crown copyright reserved

Follow this track to the next farm, pass to the right of the buildings and the road becomes tarmac. Follow this access road until just past a double wooden pylon on the right, then cross the stile on the left and walk to the far right hand corner of the field where there is another stile. Over it turn sharp left down an enclosed footpath, which turns left and then right to reach a street. Walk down this to the far end and turn right to the main road then left. Just before the roundabout cross the dual carriageway and take the cycleway opposite. Soon you are walking parallel to the motorway again. Cross the railway by the level crossing and turn left under the motorway into Pontefract Park.

Turn right along the fenced track still parallel to the motorway. When the track bears left away from the motorway keep straight on along the narrower path along the right hand edge of a wood. Soon the wood is left behind and you follow a field boundary. Cross a footbridge over a drainage channel and follow the headland path forward. When you reach the next field corner the main path turns right. Standing with your back to the motorway, two footpaths head across the field from this point. Take the one going half left, which passes well to the left of the large pylon and reaches the drainage ditch again. Ignoring the footbridge ahead, turn right along the right hand side of the drain. When you reach a cross drainage ditch keep straight on up the track to Park Grange Farm and there turn left along the track with the buildings on your right.

About 100 yards along look for a footpath forking half right off the track, which leads along the left hand edge of the golf course. When you pick up a hedge, keep to the right of it until you reach the track on the edge of the racecourse. According to the map the right of way crosses the racecourse here, although there is no sign of it and you must duck under the rails on each side. On the far side turn right along the tarmac track for 20 yards and you should see two footpaths heading out over the grass. Ignore the one making for the grandstands and take the one to the left of it. When you reach a clear cross path, go right for a short distance then fork left again and make for the football pitches.

These are on two levels: walk along the top of the embankment between them, all the way to the boating lake. Walk anticlockwise round this and at the far end go up a few steps and bear right up the broad tarmac drive. Pass to the left of the pitch and putt course and the children's playground, pass through the railings and cross the racecourse and keep forward to pass through another barrier and reach an access road. Car drivers will turn right to return to the car park, train passengers turn left, keep straight on at the roundabout to pass the gateposts, pass through the gates out of the park, cross the dual carriageway on the left, turn right for a few yards then left down the first street to return to the station.

The Ramblers' Association

*What do **we** do?*

- We work non-stop to protect footpaths.
- We campaign for more freedom of access to mountain, moorland, woodland and other open country.
- We defend the beauty and diversity of Britain's countryside.

Sixty years of successful lobbying at local and national level have been entirely dependent on membership subscriptions, donations and legacies.

We are a registered charity with over 120,000 members working hard to promote the health and educational benefits of walking in the countryside.

The **West Riding Area** is one of the 51 Areas of the Ramblers' Association which cover England, Wales and Scotland. It includes the whole of West Yorkshire and parts of North Yorkshire around Selby, York, Harrogate, Ripon, Skipton and Settle, as well as the southern part of the Yorkshire Dales National Park. The Area has over 4.000 members and is divided into 13 Local Groups.

*What can **you** do?*

If you use and enjoy the footpath network, please remember what the Ramblers' Association has done to make this possible and help us to protect it, by becoming a member now. For further information write either to

Mrs Dora Tattersall, West Riding Area Membership Secretary, 10 Woodvale Grove, Lidget Green, Bradford BD7 2SL

or The Ramblers' Association, 1/5 Wandsworth Road, London SW8 2XX.

PURSTON PARK TO EAST HARDWICK AND ACKWORTH
WALK 13

10½ miles (17 km); Pathfinder 704; easy walking through pleasantly rural countryside with fine views, with a long stretch of pleasant path by the River Went. Purston Hall (a large mansion built in the 1820s and now Featherstone Town Hall) and Park are on the southern edge of Featherstone on the B6421 Ackworth road; there are a lake and children's playground. A glance at the map will show that this walk can easily be divided into two shorter circuits. The more western of these is described in more detail (but in the opposite direction) in a leaflet published by Wakefield Countryside Service called "Two easy to follow walks around Purston & Ackworth". At times the paddock at Hessle Farm can be excessively muddy.

By bus: No. 145, 148, 149, 150 Wakefield-Pontefract, 176, 177, 178, 179 Castleford-Pontefract, 245 Pontefract-Barnsley to the junction of the Pontefract and Ackworth Roads in Featherstone. Walk along the Ackworth Road for 200 yards to Purston Park.

By car: Purston Park car park off the Ackworth Road in Purston Jaglin.

From the entrance to Purston Park walk along the B6421 Ackworth road, but when it bends right fork left into Wentbridge Road, then immediately right into Wellgarth Road. Where this ends take the footpath on the right into a field and follow the right hand edge of the field along to a cross track. Turn left along this and follow it all the way to Castle Syke Farm, where it ends. But keep forward along the left hand edge of the field to cross a stile by a gateway onto the A628 Pontefract-Barnsley road. Turn right along the footway.

In 100 yards at the road junction cross the road to look at the Ackworth Plague Stone, associated with an outbreak of plague in 1645, then cross back and continue along the footway, following the boundary wall of Ackworth Park. Pass the ruined lodge at the entrance to the Park, and about 300 yards further on look out for a public footpath sign in the hedge on the left pointing up a few steps. Two rights of way at right angles to each other cross the field from this point. Take the one bearing slightly left (we shall return by the other). On the far side pass through the hedge and cross a footbridge, then keep along the right hand edge of the next field. At its end there is another footbridge, then keep forward again along the field boundary. Cross another footbridge at the end of this field and turn sharp left with a hedge to your left. When the hedge ends at a field corner, turn right, keeping the field boundary on your left, and follow it round until a clear path heads off right across the middle of

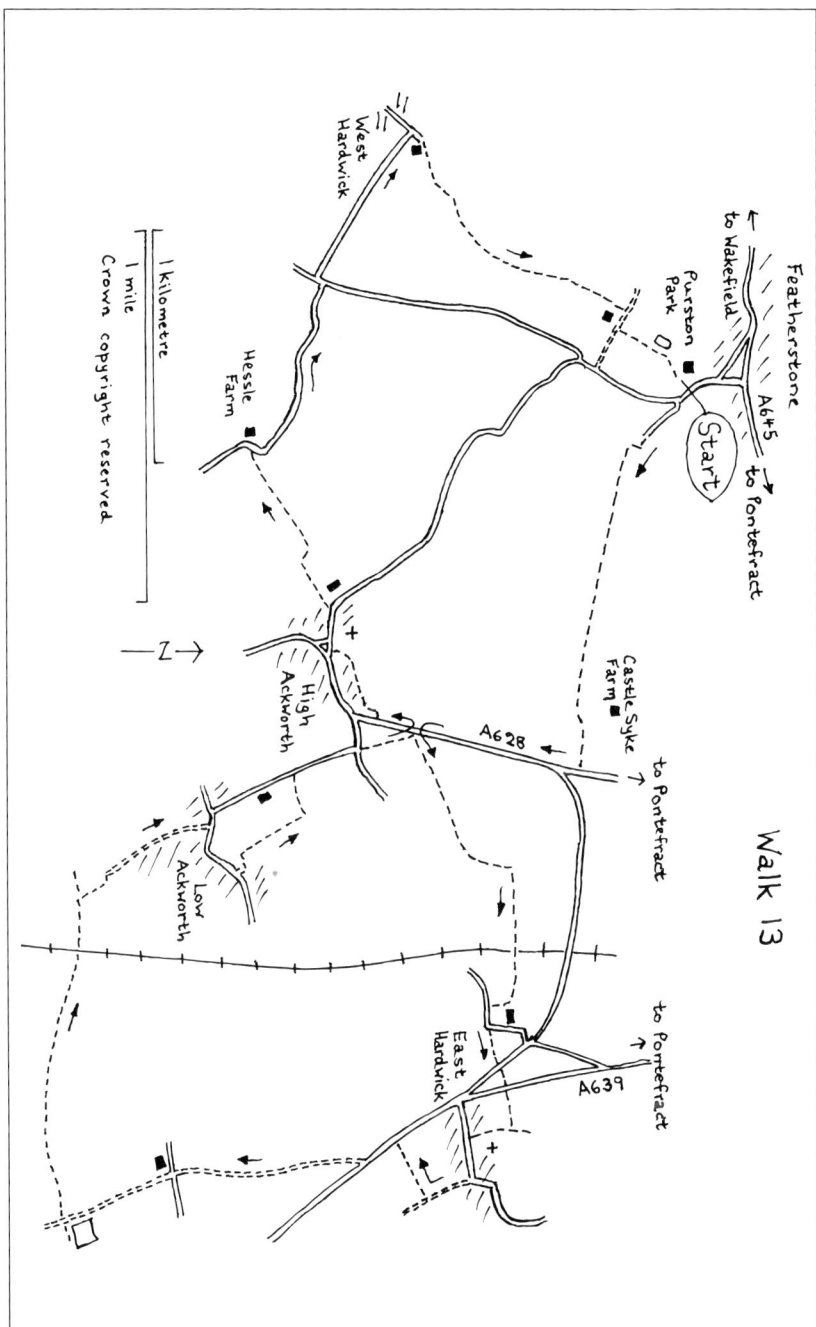

Walk 13

West Hardwick

Featherstone

to Wakefield
A645

Purston Park

Start

to Pontefract

Hessle Farm

Castle Syke Farm

to Pontefract

A628

High Ackworth

—Z→

Low Ackworth

East Hardwick

to Pontefract

A639

1 kilometre
1 mile
Crown copyright reserved

39

the field making for a footbridge in the distance. Follow the path across two fields to this bridge and cross it, then keep forward along the track. When you reach the houses of Hundhill, follow the boundary fence round to the right, to cross a stile onto Hundhill Lane. Turn left, but when the road bends left go through the gap-stile in the wall ahead and follow the fenced path to the next road. Turn left for a few yards to a stile on the right, and follow the hedge on your left to the next stile, then walk forward to the A639. Cross straight over to the footpath signpost opposite, then walk straight over the field. At the far side turn right along an old hedged track which leads to East Hardwick. The church can be visited from this track. On reaching the road turn left, but where the road begins to curve left take the bridleway on the right, an unsurfaced track.

In a little more than 200 yards cross a stile by a gate on the right and follow the hedge on your right along. Where it ends, keep straight on over the field to a stile back onto the A639. Turn left along this busy road (there is no footway) for just over 200 yards, then take the lane forking right. Look out for a fork by a small cairn and a young conifer and keep left. Soon you are walking along an attractive tree-lined avenue Cross straight over the next motor road and follow the concrete road opposite. Just before you reach the Ackworth Water Treatment Works a stone on the left informs you "Here ends Ackworth Bridle Road". Pass the entrance into the works and follow the track to the concrete bridge over the River Went. Notice the old stone packhorse bridge (Burnhill Bridge) just to the left of it.

Don't cross the bridge, but turn right along a footpath with the river to your left. There now follows a long stretch of pleasant riverside path. Having passed under a high railway viaduct keep on by the river. Pass a concrete bridge and join a track. At a fork keep right along the track, ignoring a footbridge, stile and the continuation of the riverside path. The track leads to Low Ackworth and on reaching the houses it becomes a tarmac street. When you reach the main road turn right. The road makes a long curve left, but where it begins to curve right, just after a bus shelter, post box and telephone kiosk, fork left up Westfield Grove. The track soon bends left and you reach a stile by a gate on the right.

Walk straight over the field to the stile opposite, then on by the left hand edge of the next field to the next stile. Over it turn sharp left, still with the fence/hedge on your left, to a stile and a minor road. Turn right and follow the road (Lee Lane) to High Ackworth. On reaching a T-junction, cross straight over to the stile opposite and follow the hedge/fence on your left. When the fence turns left keep straight forward across the field to the signpost visible in the far hedge. You have been here before! Go down the steps onto the A628, cross it and turn left.

Turn right along the first street you come to, Meadow Way, a no through road. At the T-junction go left, and at the turning circle go right along a fenced ginnel to reach a stile into a field. Follow the left hand edge of the field to another stile, from where a ginnel leads to the green in Ackworth village. Refreshments are available at the Brown Cow along to the left, but the walk continues down to the cross, where you turn right along the first motor road, Purston Lane. The road curves right and there is a signposted footpath on the left. Cross the stile and walk down the middle of the field, with Ackworth Old Hall, built in 1628 on the site of a mediaeval manor house and associated with the 17th-century highwayman John Nevison, over on your right. About two-thirds of the way down the field cross the stile in the fence on the right, walk forward a few yards to reach a track and turn left down this to a gate and bridge.

Turn right and then left with the track, up the right hand edge of two fields, to Hessle Farm. Cross the stile by the gate at the top and bear half right over the paddock to the next stile, also by a gate. Turn right along Hessle Lane and follow it to the next T-junction, there crossing the B6428 diagonally left into the road to West Hardwick.

On reaching the T-junction at West Hardwick turn right. Cross the stile to the left of the large farm gate and follow the fence on your right. Cross another stile and continue along an old paved path with a drainage channel on your left. When the field narrows, cross the drainage channel by a bridge and bear left and then right to follow a fence on the left. When the field boundary begins to curve right, cross a stile in the fence on the left and walk over some rough ground to a footbridge, crossing another bridge en route. Turn left along the bottom of the next field for a short distance until you reach a path heading straight up the middle of it. This path should also continue straight up the next field, heading to the left of the farm and of the end of a row of conifers. Pass to the left of the conifers, and when they end go right and then left round the edge of the field, leaving it in the corner and joining a cross track. Turn right along the track, passing the entrance to the farm, and at the end of the houses on the left go through the barrier into Purston Park and walk through it to the far end, which is where the walk started.

Wakefield Footpaths Group, which is affiliated to the Ramblers' Association, was formed in 1962 and now has around 250 members. Throughout the year three walks are arranged every Saturday, ranging from 7-16 miles. On alternate Wednesdays there is a 10-mile walk. From May to August 5-mile walks take place on alternate Tuesday and Wednesday evenings.

Annual events are two coach trips and three walking weekends. A new programme is issued every four months.

Further details can be obtained from the Secretary on 01924-279449 or from the Ridings Information Centre, Wakefield.

ACKWORTH CIRCULAR
WALK 14

4½ miles (7 km); Pathfinder 704; a stroll through quiet countryside, visiting a village which is a conservation area and passing two historic old halls. For more information about what can be seen on this walk consult the leaflet "Two easy to follow walks around Ackworth & Hessle" published by the Wakefield Countryside Service.

By bus: No.88 Pontefract-South Elmsall, No.245 Pontefract-Barnsley, No.249 Pontefract-Upton, No.479 Pontefract-Brackenhill to the junction of Bell Lane and Barnsley Road, Ackworth Moor Top. The walk starts from the car park a few yards down Bell Lane on the right. The 485 Wakefield-Doncaster bus could be taken to the roundabout at the junction of the Wakefield Road and Barnsley Road in High Ackworth; walk along the Barnsley Road in the Ackworth direction and turn left into Bell Lane.

By car: From the Barnsley Road in Ackworth Moor Top turn into Bell Lane to find a car park on the right.

From the car park go through the metal barrier and turn left along the tarmac path. Cross Woodhall Drive and then another road: a sign tells you that you are on the Dando Way, named after a local councillor. About 25 yards before the underpass fork right to the road and turn right along it, then take the next lane on the right, pass through Poplar Farm and follow the track, which soon passes Brackenhill Quarries on the right, where sandstone has been quarried since 1629. At Constitution Hill Farm keep straight forward along the footpath, passing to the left of a large stone barn, to a stile by a gate. Cross this and bear left, following the wall on your left down to a stile and footbridge, then walk along the paved path to the road.

Turn right, passing Hessle Hall, a fine manor house built in 1641. When the road turns sharp left at a large group of farm buildings, ignore the stile straight ahead, and continue on the road through Hessle Farm, then fork right off it to follow the farmyard wall to a stile by a large gate. Bear slightly right over the field to the next stile, then walk straight down the track with a fence to your left, towards Ackworth Church tower in the distance. Follow the track to the beck and cross the concrete bridge. Go through the gate on the far side and walk forward for a few yards before bearing half right to a stile in the fence. Turn left and follow the path up the field to a stile in the top left hand corner, passing Ackworth Old Hall, built in the early 1600s as a manor house on the Nostell Priory estate.

Turn right along Purston Lane into High Ackworth, a Conservation Area. When you reach the green, refreshments can be had straight ahead at the Brown Cow, on the left is Ackworth Cross, but our route turns right just before the green and descends to cross the main road and follow a ginnel immediately to the right of the almshouses opposite, built in 1741 "for a schoolmaster and six poor women". Follow the path to a turning circle at the end of a cul de sac and turn right, in a few yards turning left at the T-junction. Ignore the next street on the right and at the next T-junction keep straight ahead on a footpath between houses no.45 and 47 to a stile.

Cross straight over the middle of the field to a stile, then bear slightly left over the next field, aiming to the left of a large ash tree, to the stile by the houses. Walk forward to the road and cross diagonally right to a stile opposite into playing fields and follow the field boundary on the left. Pass a redundant stile and continue with the hedge to the left. The next stile is also redundant, as is the next one, hidden in the hedge. Walk straight across the middle of the next field to the bridge over the infant River Went opposite, but before it turn back sharp right and follow the track to Low Farm, through the farmyard and on down the access road, crossing the Went once more. At the next motor road turn left, pass a children's play area, and a short distance after passing Hillside Road on the right turn right along the cycle track signposted to Kinsley and Hemsworth. Pass under the A628 and the car park is on the left.

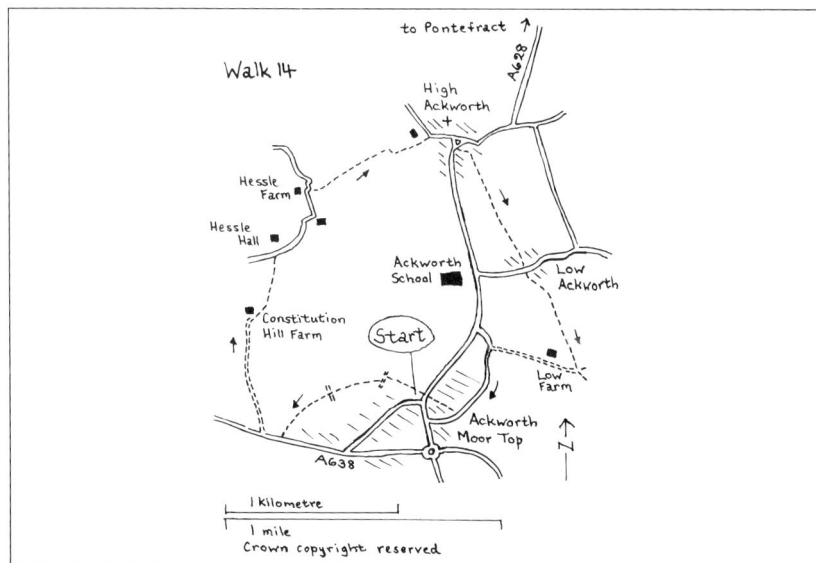

to Pontefract ↑

Walk 14

High Ackworth ✝

A628

Hessle Farm ■

Hessle Hall ●

Ackworth School ■

Low Ackworth

Constitution Hill Farm

Start

Low Farm

Ackworth Moor Top

A638

N

1 kilometre

1 mile

43

ACKWORTH, BADSWORTH AND ROYD MOOR
WALK 15

7¼ miles (11¾ km); Pathfinder 704. An easy and attractive ramble through spacious arable countryside, with wide views.

By bus: No.88 Pontefract-South Elmsall, No.245 Pontefract-Barnsley, No.249 Pontefract-Upton, No.479 Pontefract-Brackenhill to the junction of Bell Lane and Barnsley Road, Ackworth Moor Top. The walk starts from the car park a few yards down Bell Lane on the right. The 485 Wakefield-Doncaster bus could be taken to the roundabout at the junction of the Wakefield Road and Barnsley Road in High Ackworth; walk along the Barnsley Road in the Ackworth direction and turn left into Bell Lane.

By car: From the Barnsley Road in Ackworth Moor Top turn into Bell Lane to find a car park on the right.

Go through the barrier at the back of the car park and turn right along the old railway line, passing through the tunnel under the road. At the next road turn left, and follow it until you pass a recreation ground on the left. When the road begins to bend left, cross it and take the signposted track on the right. Pass to the right of Low Farm and follow the track over the next field to a stone bridge. Cross it and walk half left over the next field to cross a stile and footbridge in the far hedge, then walk up the middle of the next field towards the left hand end of Moor House Farm. Cross the stile by the corner of the barn and walk diagonally over the next field to the stile in the far corner. Turn left through the tunnel under the railway.

The track bears right and ends at a sort of turning circle. Bear right here on a clear path towards a double wooden pylon. On reaching the scant remains of a hedge at the next field corner, keep forward to the right of the hedge, pass to the right of the pylon and a few yards further on go left with the field boundary. A little later follow it right again. In the next corner cross the stile and follow the path forward through the trees. Pass to the right of the first house, ignore a footpath sign pointing right, and keep forward along the track, which at Nineveh Farm becomes a surfaced road. Climb to Badsworth. Just over the brow of the hill you reach a crossroads. Ignore Main Street on the left and keep forward along Back Lane.

Just after a large stone barn on the left (ripe for conversion!) a footpath leads down the front of New Row, if you want to visit the church, otherwise keep on for another 60 yards and take the signposted

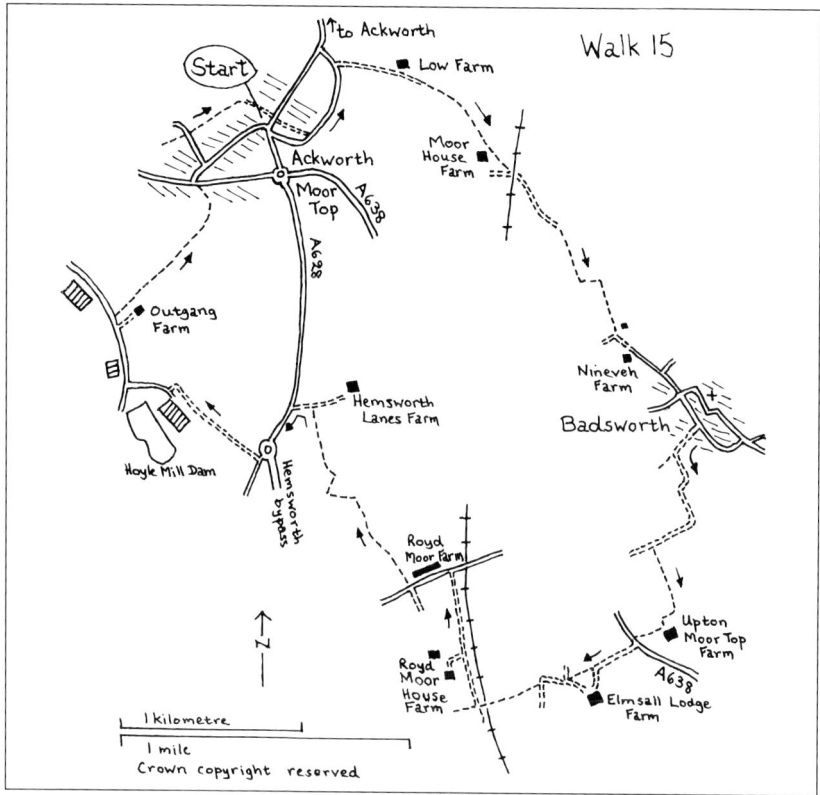

Walk 15

lane on the right. When the surface ends, keep on along the hedged track, which soon ends at a large double gate. Go through the kissing-gate beside this and turn left along the track. It soon curves right, then left, and then turns sharp right. About 250 yards after this turn, turn sharp left off the track across the field (the path should be clear) to a marker post on the far side. Now bear very slightly right along the field boundary towards Upton Moor Top Farm. On the far side of this field there is another marker post. Turn right along the left hand edge of the field with the hedge on the left to an old kissing-gate buried in it.

Turn sharp left here towards the farm, pass to the right of a barn and turn sharp right along the edge of the field with a fence and wood on your left. In the bottom corner cross a footbridge and pass the remains of another metal kissing-gate to reach the A638.

Cross diagonally left and follow the access road to Elmsall Lodge Farm. When the road curves left to the farm, keep straight forward across the field. On the far side leave the field and turn right along a

45

cross track (i.e. don't turn sharp right along the track in the field you have just crossed). When the hedge on the left turns left, go with it for a couple of yards then bear half right on a clear path across the field. This leads in a straight line to a bridge over a railway. Immediately after this turn right along a hedged track and follow this to the next road, being joined on the way by the access track from Royd Moor House Farm.

Cross the road and turn left, pass Royd Moor Farm, where the footway ends, and continue along the verge for 70 yards to a signposted stile on the right. Once in the field go left for a few yards then turn right on a clear path on a field boundary, passing to the right of a double wooden pylon. There are very extensive views. The field boundary suddenly ends at a footpath signpost. Here the right of way makes a dog leg (but look out for a diversion to remove it!), so turn left and walk to another signpost in the next field boundary and there turn right, keeping a ditch on your left, to follow the field edge along to the next corner, where there is a double footbridge on the left and another footpath sign. Bear slightly right over the next very large field, if possible using a convenient tractor trail. You should hit the far side of the field about 200 yards to the left of the farm. Turn left along the track to the A628.

Turn left along the footway, cross the road when convenient, and walk anti-clockwise round the roundabout at the start of the Hemsworth bypass. Take the first road on the right for 25 yards, then turn right along the bridleway, passing through a small metal gate beside a large double one. Follow the track over the field. Pass to the right of a turkey farm and follow the track as it curves left to join a surfaced road. Turn right along it. At the next T-junction turn right again, passing to the right of another turkey farm. As you draw level with a tall wooden pylon on the left of the road turn right through the hedge and follow the clear path across the middle of the large field, with Outgang Farm on your right.

On reaching the far side of the field, go through the old hedgerow and cross the next, much smaller field, then walk along the left hand edge of the next one. Where the field edge curves right, go straight on out of the field and bear left to the end of the wooden fence which faces you, where you will find a hedged footpath. Where this ends, walk diagonally right over a small patch of grass to pick up a fenced tarmac path which leads to the right of the cricket ground to the busy A638. Cross it and fork right down Bell Lane. On reaching an altered road junction turn left along Hardaker Lane. Just after Banks Avenue on the left turn right through the barrier and follow the tarmac path along the right hand edge of a broad strip of grass. Cross a street and follow the path opposite back to your starting point.

UPTON, BADSWORTH AND THORPE AUDLIN
WALK 16

6 miles (9½ km); Pathfinder 704; easy, almost level walking through attractive arable countryside with some fine views. For more information about what can be seen on this walk consult the leaflet "Two easy to follow walks around Thorpe Audlin & Badsworth" published by the Wakefield Countryside Service

By bus: No. 485 Wakefield-Doncaster, No. 246 Pontefract-Barnsley to Quarry Lane on the northern side of Upton, not far from the Beacon.

By car: From Wakefield follow the A638 Doncaster Road to Ackworth and continue along it until you reach a road on the left signposted to Badsworth. Turn second right at Badsworth along Main Street and follow the road to Upton. About 200 yards after the start of the 30 mph limit at Upton Beacon turn left into Quarry Lane and park on the verge beside the high boundary fence of the sports fields. Walk back to the main road and turn right.

Follow the main road back to the end of the 30 mph limit and fork right along a hedged track (bridleway sign). Upton Beacon is to your right, and there are fine views left and ahead as you emerge from the hedged lane: Badsworth is down on your left and Thorpe Audlin ahead and slightly to the right, with Pontefract the town in the distance. Keep forward down the path between fields, at the bottom cross through the old hedgerow, and now you have a hedge on your left. When this ends, keep on, and just before reaching Rogerthorpe Manor you pick up another hedge, this time on your right.

Go through the gate ahead and follow the path, which bears slightly left, over the next field to join the boundary fence of the Manor, built around 1600 and now a country house hotel. At the road turn left, ignoring the track opposite, and in 100 yards fork right through a kissing-gate and follow the left hand edge of two fields to enter an enclosed path which leads to the churchyard of Badsworth Church.

Follow the path round past the front of the church, ignoring the entrance gate on the left, past the church door and out onto the road. Turn right. Follow the road left, with all that remains of Badsworth Hall ahead, then take the first lane on the right (Nineveh Lane). Walk down the hill and turn right along the unsurfaced Grove Lane. After passing a large barn on the right of the track fork right, then when you reach a cross track turn left and follow this track to a bridge over the River Went, here just a beck. Notice the older bridge on the right. Turn right along a footpath by the river, immediately crossing a stone footbridge, and follow the riverside path as far as the next footbridge over the river.

Cross this and walk straight up the field towards the houses of Thorpe Audlin. As you reach them, the path becomes a track. Cross straight over a road, to follow the footpath opposite. Cross straight over the main road by the bus shelter in Thorpe Audlin and take the minor road opposite, Darning Lane. At the next crossroads turn right down Causeway Garth Lane, passing Thorpe Manor over a high wall on the left. Where the tarmac lane bends left, keep straight on down the unsurfaced track signposted to Upton. The track turns right and then left and after a time turns right again for a yard or two, crosses a ditch and ends at a large field. There should be a clear path heading half left across it.

At the far side turn left, keeping the field boundary on your right. At the far end cross the footbridge on the right and turn left. Ignore the footbridge ahead and follow the field edge round to the right until you reach another footbridge on the left. Cross this. The path on the left leads through the Pothills Marsh nature reserve, managed by Wakefield Council (see Walk 17), but we turn right, pass through the field boundary and then bear left up the left hand edge of the next field. At the top turn right with the hedge for 20 yards to find a stile on the left. Cross it and walk up the right hand edge of the next field with a wood to your right. Cross the stile at the top and walk up the hedged lane. The lane begins to descend and you join a high fence on the right. Follow this round to the right and you are in Quarry Lane, which leads back to the starting point.

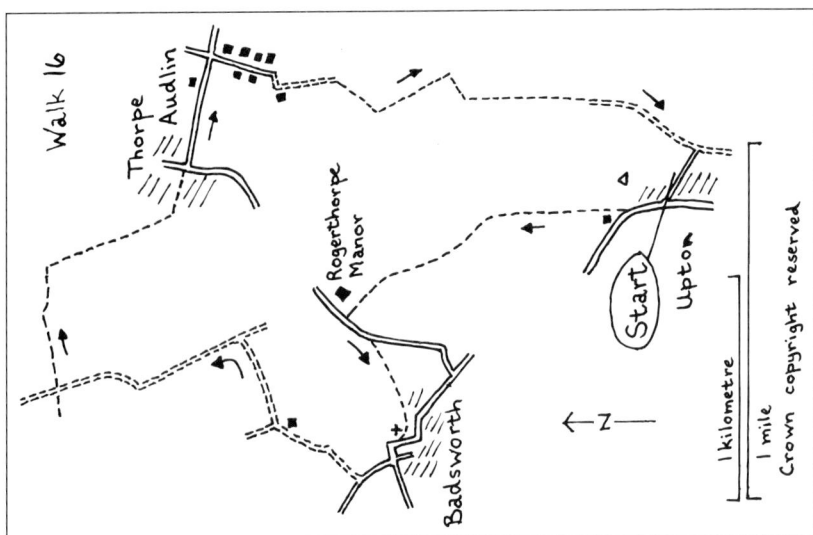

UPTON AND BULLCAR MIRES
WALK 17

5 miles (8 km); Pathfinder 704. A walk through a reclaimed colliery, a nature reserve and limestone woodland; fine views. Just outside the car park at the start of the walk is a memorial to the miners who lost their lives in Upton Colliery 1926-1964.

By bus: 246 Pontefract-Barnsley, 249 Pontefract-Upton, 485 Wakefield-Doncaster to the Upton Centre on Waggon Lane, then walk back towards the centre of Upton and turn left into the car park of the Upton Colliery Reclamation Site.

By car: A car park has been laid out for access to the reclaimed Upton Colliery on Waggon Lane, Upton. Park here.

Leave the car park through the barrier and take the left hand path towards a bench and litter bin, with the lake down on the right. Cross a stone bridge and fork right, and at the next fork keep left past another bench and litter bin. At the next fork turn right to pass over another stone bridge, and immediately after the bridge keep straight on at the junction of tracks. The track passes to the right of an old winding wheel, which has been set up as a monument. At the next junction take the right hand path, that is keep straight on through trees. The track descends and curves right to a very clear cross track: cross straight over, towards the remains of a brick railway bridge, but turn left just before them to walk along the bottom of the railway embankment. Soon follow a path which forks right up onto the old railway line and bear left along it.

Follow the disused railway until the clear path turns right down the embankment. At this point take another path which drops left down the embankment to cross a concrete bridge and pass through a metal barrier. Walk forward to the next street and turn right along it. It bears left to reach a T-junction: turn right, cross the road near the bus shelter, and in a few yards when the road curves right, turn left along a track, and when the houses end keep forward along a narrower track, Sheepwalk Lane. Follow it up to the top of the hill to the edge of Walton Wood and turn right along the cross track along the outside edge of the wood. A short distance along fork left on a clear path down into the wood. On leaving the wood keep down the left hand edge of the field, and at the bottom turn right along a stony track with Walton Wood House on your left.

The track bends left to reach the access drives to Walton Wood House and Walton Wood Dovecote. Leaving the entrances into these two houses on the left, walk straight forward down a track, which soon

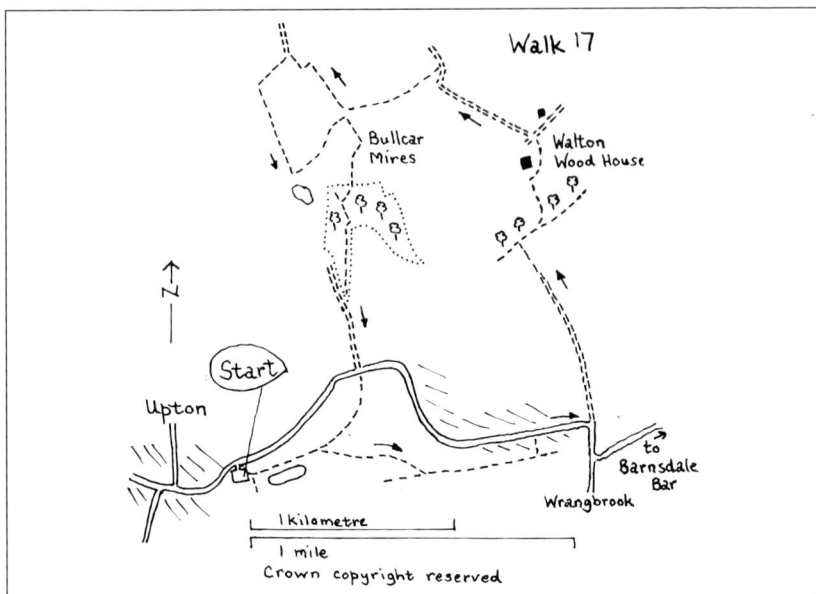

Walk 17

Bullcar Mires

Walton Wood House

N↑

Start

Upton

Wrangbrook

to Barnsdale Bar

1 Kilometre

1 mile

Crown copyright reserved

crosses the grass runway of Walton Wood airfield. On reaching the far end of the field follow the track right. (Look out for a possible diversion here: follow waymarks!) It soon turns left again and crosses a beck. Turn left again immediately, off the track, and walk back in the direction you have just come from, with the beck on your left. Just before the field boundary turns right, ignore steps and a footbridge on the left and keep along the field edge. Soon you pass to the left of a small wood. Keep along the field edge as it bends sharp left and then sharp right again. The old village of Thorpe Audlin is over half right. When you reach an old gateway on the left turn through it. The track on the right leads to Thorpe Audlin, but our route leads forward over the beck and then slightly left over the next large field.

At the far side turn left, keeping the field boundary on your right. At the far end of the field cross the footbridge on the right and turn left to cross another footbridge into Bullcar Mires SSI. We are going to follow the path essentially round the edge of the nature reserve: please don't stray from it. So take the path on the left. Wakefield Council have provided boardwalks over wet patches and have also dug out small ponds to encourage wild life. After a time you cross a footbridge and reach the steps and footbridge which you passed earlier. Turn right here (a notice shows the popular name for this nature reserve, Pothills Marsh) on the clear path through the tussocky grass with a hedge closeby on

50

the left. Soon the path leaves the hedge and makes for gorse bushes. Keep on the clearest path, which passes between gorse bushes and then along their right hand edge. Soon there is more boardwalk. At a fork go left across more boardwalk and walk along close to the left hand edge of the reserve towards Bullcar Plantation.

Enter the wood by passing through a kissing-gate and crossing a footbridge. Follow the clear path forward and when you reach a cross path turn right. Soon you reach a crossing of paths. Going right here would allow you to have a look at the wildlife on the lake, but our route turns left on the path which climbs through the wood. At the top boundary of the wood turn right along the cross track, soon reaching a bench which is a fine viewpoint. Continue along the top edge of the wood with a hedge on your left. When the path reaches a track, Green Lane, bear left up it. About 40 yards before you reach the next road fork left off the track onto an old railway line and pass through the tunnel under the road.

Turn right immediately, pass through some trees and turn sharp left to join a grit road. Ignore the metal kissing-gate on the left and follow the grit road as it curves right, then pass through the next metal kissing-gate. Go through and follow the path forward to a T-junction, where you turn right alongside the high railings. You are of course now back in the Upton Colliery Reclamation Site. Follow this path back to the car park, on the way rejoining your outward route.

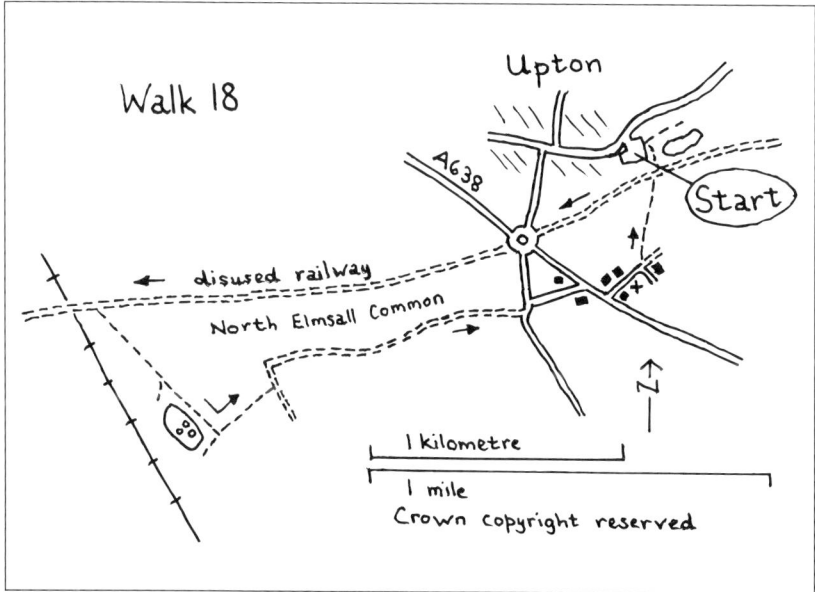

Walk 18

Upton

A638

disused railway

North Elmsall Common

Start

N

1 kilometre

1 mile

Crown copyright reserved

NORTH ELMSALL COMMON
WALK 18

3½ miles (5½ km); Pathfinder 704. An easy and delightful stroll through pleasant countryside, visiting some reclaimed land with a lake popular with water birds. The outward route is almost entirely along the line of a disused railway noted for its wild flowers and butterflies.

By bus: 246 Pontefract-Barnsley, 249 Pontefract-Upton, 485 Wakefield-Doncaster to the Upton Centre on Waggon Lane, then walk back towards the centre of Upton and turn left into the car park of the Upton Colliery Reclamation Site.

By car: A car park has been laid out for access to the reclaimed Upton Colliery on Waggon Lane, Upton. Park here.

Pass through the barrier out of the car park and turn right, keeping the lake on your left. When you reach a cross track, turn right along it. This is a former railway line, which you will follow for the outward half of the walk. Keep always to the clearest path, avoiding right forks, and eventually you will pass an old platform and soon reach a metal kissing-gate leading to a track beside a house which brings you to a roundabout on the A638. Go clockwise round the roundabout, crossing two roads, then drop steeply down to resume your walk along the railway trackbed. The next section, running through a cutting, can be wet, but it does not last long.

After a time you are quite high above the surrounding countryside. The very clear track ends where reclaimed mine workings begin. Down on the right here are two small lakes which you might like to explore, but the walk keeps forward with a fence on the left. At the top of the slope stay with the fence as it turns left to follow a broad grassy track. South Elmsall is ahead to the left, South Kirkby to the right. Soon ahead you will see a lake with three small islands, which attracts many birds. Keep forward with the lake to your right, and at the far end of it turn sharp left and walk along to the right of a double wire fence.

At the hedge on the far side turn left along a clear cross track, which in just over 100 yards turns right. Follow this track all the way to the B6274 and cross diagonally left to take the minor road opposite. On reaching the A638, cross and turn right, but in a few yards fork left along another minor road. Notice the old milestone by Milestone House on the right. Pass the church of St. Margaret, North Elmsall, and where the road bends right cross the stile on the left and follow the clear path over the field to the next stile, then bear half right across the next field. On the far side bear left to the next stile in the hedge, which takes you back onto the old railway track you started out on. Turn right, then left just before the lake to return to your starting point.

SOUTH ELMSALL TO CLAYTON AND FRICKLEY
WALK 19

7½ miles (12 km); Pathfinder 704, 716. The juxtaposition of industrial wasteland, pleasant countryside and parkland with a glimpse of a stately home gives this walk variety.

By train: to South Elmsall (Metro Train Wakefield Line).

By car: car park at South Elmsall Station.

Walk to the far end of the station car park and a few yards after passing a large brick shed on the left turn right through the bushes and down some steps and ignoring the footbridge ahead turn left along the grass with the beck to your right. Cross the next footbridge, with a kissing-gate before it, and walk up the following street to the main road. Turn left. When the houses and the 30 mph limit end, cross the road and take the track leading in a few yards to a metal barrier by a large gate. Follow the broad grassy track leading forward from the gate and climbing gently, and at the top of the slope choose the track bearing slightly left. Follow it over the reclaimed colliery waste until it descends to another large metal gate with a barrier beside it. Turn right along the road with a spoil heap on your right..

Having passed under an old railway bridge fork left along the hedged Frickley Lane, soon entering South Yorkshire, and quickly the landscape changes. Pass a pair of brick semis, set back on the right, and keep forward into Frickley Park. At the T-junction turn right, cross a cattle-grid, look left for a glimpse of the 18th-century Frickley Hall, and keep forward on the tarmac road. At a crossroads go straight on, and after a time walk straight through the yard of the Home Farm. When the track swings right, stay with it, passing to the left of a stone built house and soon crossing the railway. Just after the bridge ignore a track forking left. Ignore the next track on the right to Wink House. A little further on a signpost on the left indicates a path to Clayton, visited on walk 22.

Barely 200 yards beyond that at a wide junction where several tracks meet, turn right along the signposted track between hedges, obviously a route of some antiquity, judging by the causeyed path on the left of the track. After a time the track narrows to a hedged footpath, and shortly after passing a large pylon on the right (ignore the marker post here) the path curves right into a field. Walk along the right hand edge of this, turn left with it at the far end, ignoring a gap on the right into the next field, cross Howell Beck by a footbridge and return into Wakefield District.

Ahead of you is a spoil heap, but immediately after the bridge turn left on a clear path which soon bears right away from the beck and

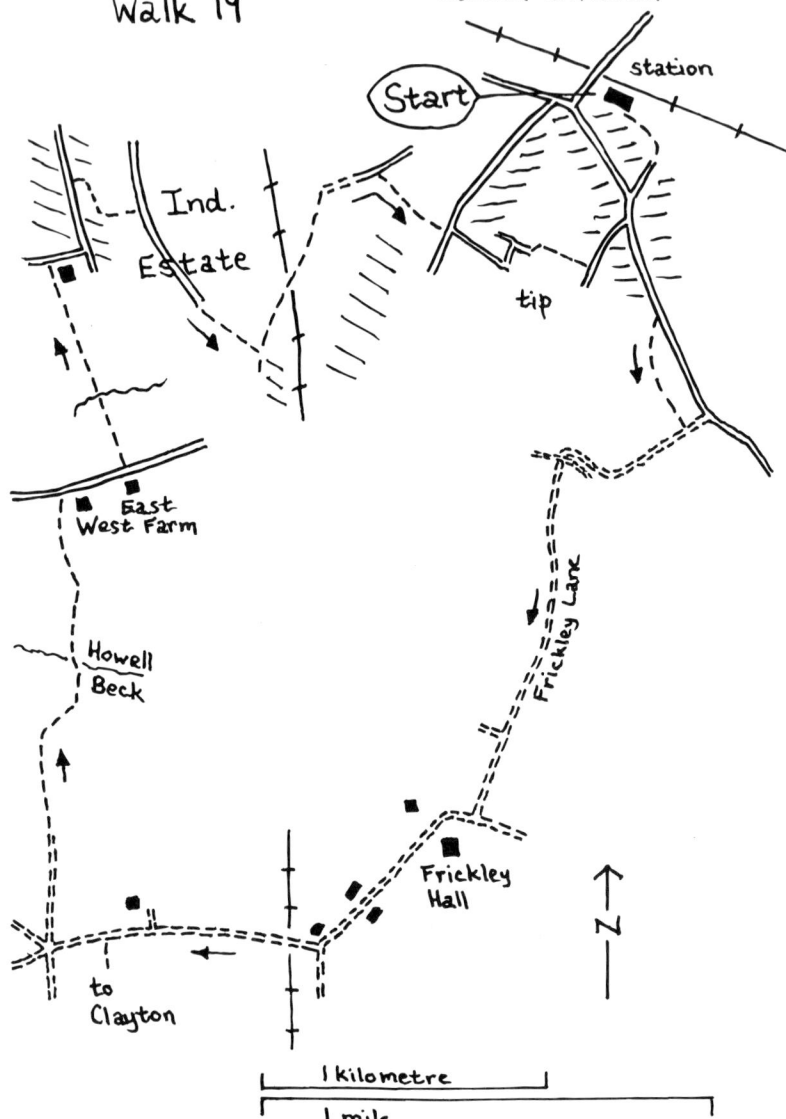

Walk 19

South Elmsall

Start

station

Ind. Estate

tip

East West Farm

Howell Beck

Frickley Lane

Frickley Hall

N →

to Clayton

1 kilometre

1 mile

Crown copyright reserved

follows the boundary fence of the mine. After a time you walk along the right hand edge of a field and join a track. On reaching a track on the right leading to West Farm, keep straight forward over the field to a stile in the hedge ahead. Turn right along Broad Lane, passing West Farm, but when you are opposite the next farm, East Farm, turn left over a stile and walk along the right hand edge of the field. At the far end turn left for a few yards, then right to cross Langthwaite Beck, then keep forward with a fence on your right and Langthwaite Grange Industrial Estate beyond.

On reaching the houses keep forward along a track, which passes to the left of Burntwood Infants School. Turn right when you reach the road, cross over the next street (Church Top), turn left at the end, then between houses 144 and 145 on the right go through a ginnel with a barrier at each end and fork right along a tarmac path, soon with the fence of the Industrial Estate on your left. The path turns left between high fences. On reaching the next road turn right along it and follow it through the Estate all the way to its end, then continue forward along a tarmac footpath. Cross the canalised Langthwaite Beck, then cross a concrete footbridge over the former bed of the beck and turn left over the grass with the beck on your left. Turn left along a cross path which crosses Langthwaite Beck yet again.

The path crosses the railway by a high footbridge and continues between hedges. When the hedged path ends you pass a pub called Little John's Well and join a road for about 100 yards to take a tarmac footpath on the right. A few yards along ignore a right fork, a few yards further ignore a left fork through bollards, and keep on along the back of a row of houses. The path climbs gently and becomes enclosed. Follow it up to Westfield Lane, which you reach by the Westfield Hotel. Cross the road diagonally left and go down Oxford Street opposite. At the far end turn left, ignore a lane on the right leading to a garage, cross over the next street and pass between the houses on the far side, and then with an iron fence ahead turn right. In a few yards steps lead down half left.

Follow the tarmac path along the bottom of the houses and at the lamppost at the end fork right along an unsurfaced path, which leads along with a hedge on the left and a ditch and spoil heap on the right. When you emerge onto a street, turn left along it, and on reaching the main road, cross it and turn left. You are now back on your outward route. Turn right along Palmers Avenue, follow it to the end, keep forward to cross the footbridge and turn left over the grass with the beck to your left. When you reach another footbridge turn right up the steps, then left into the station car park.

SOUTH ELMSALL TO HOOTON PAGNELL
WALK 20

7¾ miles (12½ km); Pathfinder 704, 716. Quiet arable and wooded countryside, mainly in South Yorkshire, and visiting an attractive limestone village. After rain the surface of some of the paths can be slippery mud.

By train: to South Elmsall (Metro Train Wakefield Line).

By car: car park at South Elmsall Station.

If coming by train from Wakefield you will need to climb the long flight of steps, cross the railway by the road bridge and descend the steps on the other side into the station car park. Walk to the far end of the car park and continue along the road parallel to the railway. Follow it until you are faced by the gates of South Elmsall Waste Water Treatment Works. Here turn right and follow the fence down, turning left with it at the bottom and following the path across a wooden footbridge to enter South Yorkshire. Turn left along the field edge for a few yards until a drainage ditch comes across the field from the right. Turn right here and walk along the left side of this ditch to the far side of the field, there going right over a small footbridge and in a few yards left over another footbridge and up some steps to cross a disused railway line. On the far side cross the cross track diagonally right, descend the steps, cross another little bridge and a stile, and walk straight over the field to Moorhouse Grange Farm.

Turn left to follow the boundary fence/hedge of the farm, and when the hedge turns right, go half right over the field to a road. Turn left along it. Ignore a footpath sign pointing right at Moorhouse Equestrian Centre, but shortly after the houses end fork right off the road up a track. Cross straight over the next road and follow the well-used footpath across the large field, passing what looks like a redundant stile on the way. Cross the field boundary at the top and walk along the left hand edge of three fields to reach a cross track. Turn left for a few yards to another cross track and turn right along it. This is marked on the map "Old Street".

Having passed a wood, ignore a track on the right and keep forward until you reach a signposted junction shortly before the next wood. Turn right here and follow the track ("Narrow Balk") to Hooton Pagnell. On reaching the next cross track on the edge of the village turn left for a few yards then go right through a gateway and follow the track forward, passing through another gateway, to reach the road in the village centre. Notice the plaque opposite, which informs you that beyond the wall is

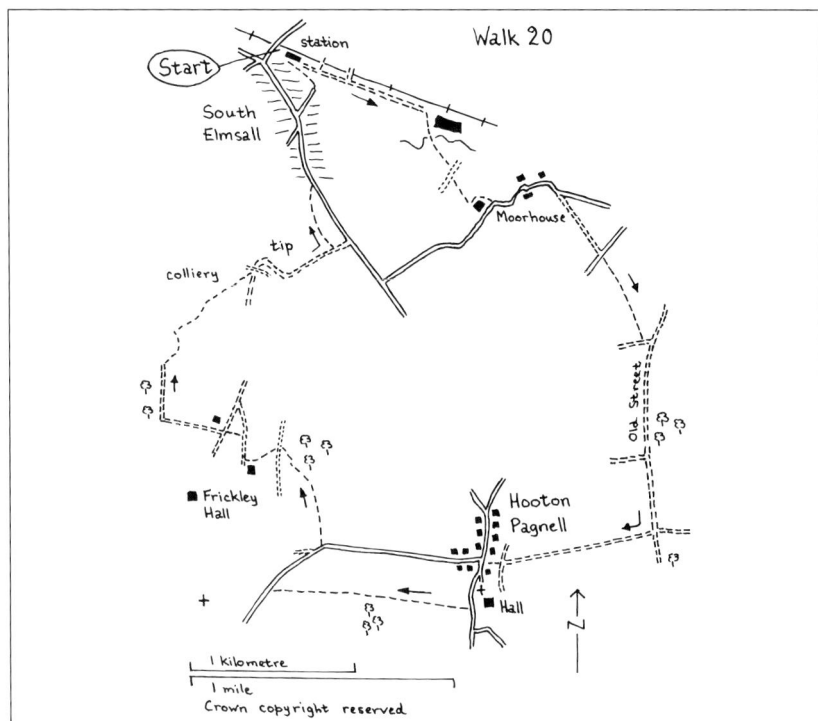

Walk 20

the village pound, and behind the Butter Cross, erected between 1540 and 1550, is another plaque which states that the village was given its market charter in 1253 by Henry III. It is worth having a stroll through this delightful village.

Our route turns left to the churchyard, entered through the lych-gate. Pass to the left round the church and you will glimpse ahead Hooton Pagnell Hall, which dates from Tudor times. Turn right to the entrance to the church, a fine example of Norman architecture. Bear left down the steps - there are benches here which invite you to pause and enjoy the view westwards - then descend some more steps to the road. Walk along it past the 14th-century gatehouse of the Hall (notice the carriage and pedestrian entrances).

In 100 yards turn right over the signposted stile, and on reaching the field go left for a few yards, then turn right on a clear path across the middle. Look back for another view of the Hall. Pass to the right of a small wood and walk straight over the middle of the next field. On reaching the far side, follow the path through the wood, cross a small stone bridge and walk up to cross a stile into the next field. Walk straight across it to a marker post on the far side, cross the sleeper bridge and keep forward along the left hand edge of the next field. At the far end go left for a few yards to cross another small bridge, walk up into the next field and bear half right over it to cut the corner of the field and reach a road at a footpath sign.

Frickley Church is visible half left, Frickley Hall straight ahead. Turn right along the road and follow it for about 400 yards until just after the access drive to Frickley Hall on the left you cross a stile by a large double gate on the left and follow the track across the field. It leads to Hooton Pagnell Wood. Do not enter the wood, but take the path on the left just before it along the right hand edge of the field with the wood on the right. The path leads to a disused railway marked by trees. A few yards before this fork left round the end of the field, cross the old railway, pass a redundant stile on the far side and bear half left over the next field. Drop down through the trees on the far side, cross a beck, go through a gate and walk forward with a wall on your left. On reaching a track coming from the farm on the left, turn right along it, but at the far end of the wood on the left turn sharp left off the track and follow the edge of the wood up to a stile and another cross track (Frickley Lane).

Cross straight over and take the track opposite, passing to the left of a pair of brick semis. Follow the wood on your left and when the track turns right keep with it, still with the wood on your left. When this wood ends you cross a beck (and back into Wakefield District) and immediately turn right along a track with the beck in a deep channel on the right. Where this ditch ends, the track forks: keep left along a narrow path which soon bears left out of the wood and follows the left hand edge of a field, under power lines, to the boundary fence of a colliery. Turn right on a path which keeps just outside this fence.

Having passed through a stretch of woodland you follow the left hand edge of a field. In the far corner you re-join Frickley Lane, which comes in from the right. Turn left under the old railway bridge and follow the road round the edge of the spoil heaps. About 100 yards before you reach the B6422 turn left through a metal barrier and climb the facing slope on reclaimed colliery waste. When the grassy track forks, keep right towards the houses and follow this track to another barrier and the main road on the edge of South Elmsall. Turn left and walk through the village until you reach Palmers Avenue on the right (signposted as a public footpath), follow it to the end, keep forward to cross a footbridge and turn left over the grass with the beck to your left. When you reach another footbridge turn right up some steps, then left into the station car park.

SOUTH AND NORTH ELMSALL
WALK 21

5¼ miles (8½ km); Pathfinder 704. A walk through the pleasant countryside north-east of South Elmsall.

By train: to South Elmsall (Metro Train Wakefield Line).

By car: car park at South Elmsall Station.

Walk to the far end of the station car park and continue along the tarmac road. Cross the railway by the high footbridge and follow the concrete path up to the houses. On reaching them turn right along the bottom of their gardens and at the far end turn left up the track. Cross straight over the next street and follow the path into the field on the right and walk up the left hand edge of this to reach the next road by a double wooden pylon. Turn right along the road (Trough Lane). When the tarmac ends at Quarry Farm, keep straight forward along the track, but when this bends left, the footpath continues straight ahead on the right hand side of the field boundary. For a short distance you have a hedge on the left. When the hedge ends, keep forward over the field to the trees, turn left for a few yards then go down steep steps on the right to cross a disused railway line. Climb the steps on the other side and bear slightly left across the next field, aiming for the left hand side of a bungalow, to climb a few steps and reach the busy A638.

Cross the road and walk up the left hand side of the bungalow. At the far end of the field cross through the facing hedge and continue with a hedge to your right. When this hedge ends at a little wood, keep straight forward across the field until you reach a cross path on a narrow unploughed strip of grass. Turn left along it. Having passed under power lines cross a cross track and keep forward along the field boundary until you cross a footbridge and reach the fence of Upton Wrangbrook Waste Water Treatment Works. Bear left and shortly right along it, and at the far end turn right with the fence then climb a few steps half left onto a disused railway track and bear right along it. Pass to the left of a house, reach a junction of tracks and take the one on the left.

When the track turns right, keep straight forward to cross a stile just to the right of an enormous pylon, then continue down the right hand edge of the next field. Having crossed a stile in a facing fence, you soon cross another one onto Sleep Hill Lane. Turn left to the road junction, cross the road and enter the access drive to Brookside Farm opposite. A few yards before you reach a large gate cross a footbridge on the left, then a step-stile, and walk forward over the grass to another stile at the far end. Having crossed it, go left at a cross path, but immediately take the right fork and at the next fork keep right again, always on the main path, which soon climbs steeply up onto another former railway line. Turn left along this.

At a fork, keep left to stay on the railway line, now in a shallow cutting, but at the next fork take the main path to the right, leading off the railway line to a track, and turn left along it. The track soon reaches a cross path, which to the left crosses the railway, but we go right for a yard or two to join a broad cross track and turn left along it. It soon leads back onto the railway trackbed. Follow this through a deep cutting, at the end of which you are joined by another track from the right. Now there is a large lake on the right, part of the Upton Colliery Reclamation Site (see Walk 17) and at the far end of this another track comes in from the right.

Look out for a stile on the left just before a very large pylon in the field on the left. Walk forward across the field, about 20 yards to the left of the pylon, crossing a footbridge and then bearing half right on a well used path over the field. At the far side cross a stile and continue on the same line over the next field to another stile onto a road. Turn right along this, passing St Margaret's Church, North Elmsall, to the A638 again. Cross the road to the signposted path opposite. A clear path bears half left over the next field to a stile, from which you bear very slightly left over the next field to another stile, and again bear slightly left across the next field to a ladder-stile in the corner. Keep the same line over the next field to a stile in the far corner out onto the B6474.

Cross the road and turn left to the traffic lights, cross to the Barnsley Oak opposite and turn right down Minsthorpe Lane. Just after the bus shelter on the left turn left along Bailey Crescent, then take the first street on the right, Hutton Drive. Follow it to the far end, cross Ash Grove and turn left, to pass Minsthorpe Swimming Pool and Ash Grove School. Having passed Trinity Methodist Church on the other side of the road turn right down the High Street to return to South Elmsall Station.

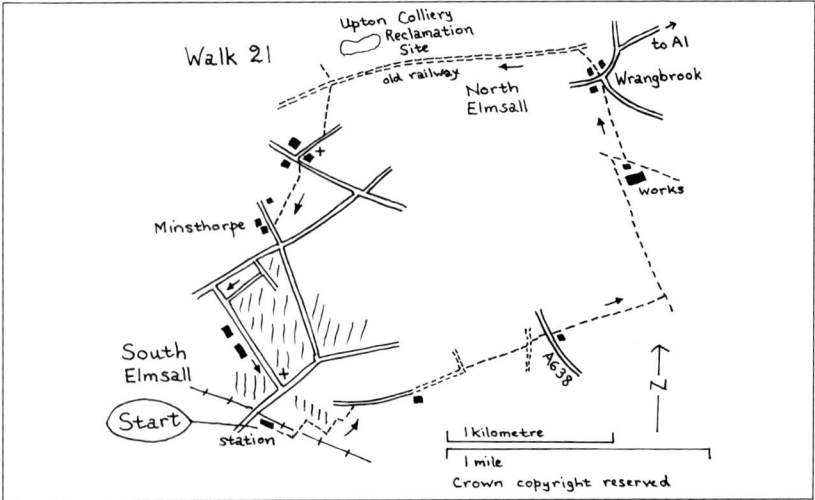

MOORTHORPE TO CLAYTON
WALK 22

6¼ miles (10 km); Pathfinder 704, 716. Another striking transition from industrial dereliction to peaceful undulating arable countryside, with a delightful village at the halfway point.

By train: _The walk starts at Moorthorpe Station (Metro Wakefield Line). Passengers from Wakefield will need to cross the line by the crossing to reach the car park._

By car: _Park at Moorthorpe Station._

Walk out of the car park past the Mallard pub to the main road and turn left, crossing the railway bridge. Cross the road when convenient, and immediately after passing the Miners' Institute turn right down Wesley Street. At the foot turn right again and follow the track to the right of Little John's Well pub. After the pub keep forward along the track, which soon turns left and becomes hedged. The track crosses the railway by a high bridge. Cross a little footbridge and keep forward, crossing over a cross path, and keep forward along the hedged path to a road. Turn left for just over 100 yards to a signposted track on the right just before another railway bridge. The track keeps parallel to the railway, soon with mine workings on the right.

Follow the railway, after a time high on an embankment, until the end of the mine on the right, when the track curves right past a tall pylon and narrows to a footpath, parallel to the power lines. At a crossing of paths turn left through the wood. Cross a beck (here entering South Yorkshire and passing from an industrial to a rural landscape), pass between two old stone gateposts and walk forward across the field on a track to the hedge opposite. Pass through the hedge and keep forward to the right of another hedge which curves up towards Wink House Farm. Stay by the hedge until you reach a stile in a fence. Cross it and walk straight across the next field to a stile by a gate opposite, then continue through the next field, passing to the left of the farm, to a stile in the far right hand corner.

Cross and turn right along the track, with Clayton over to your left. After 150 yards cross the signposted stile on the left and walk towards Clayton with the hedge on your right. At the far end of the field cross the stile by the gate, then Frickley Beck, and walk up the lane into the village. On reaching the road, the War Memorial is on the left, the village pond, where there are benches, on the right. Turn right through the village, which has some charming old houses, including the brick Manor

Farm and the stone Old Hall Farm. Ignore Hall Brig forking right, but just after Paddock Cottage on the right cross the stile by the gate and walk down the field with the hedge on your right to a barrier in the bottom corner, from which a paved path leads forward.

Climb the steps to the next road and turn left. Follow this tarmac lane through and out of the village, and where it turns left, turn right along a track. When you reach a cross track, keep forward into the field and walk down with the hedge on your right through this field and the next one. Cross a stile in the hedge onto a track and turn left. After 50 yards ignore a track going right, signposted as a public footpath, and keep straight on (signposted public bridleway). A few yards after the track bends right ignore another track forking off left. After a time the track narrows to a headland footpath. Cross Howell Beck by a footbridge (re-entering the Wakefield District). The remains of the old hedged way are still visible, but walkers have created a new path to the right of it.

When you reach the end of the old field boundary on the left, ignore the path straight ahead across the middle of the field and turn sharp left for a short distance, then right again, and now you are back in the old hedged way. Follow this all the way to the next road, Broad Lane, and turn right for 40 yards. About four yards after the first isolated tree on

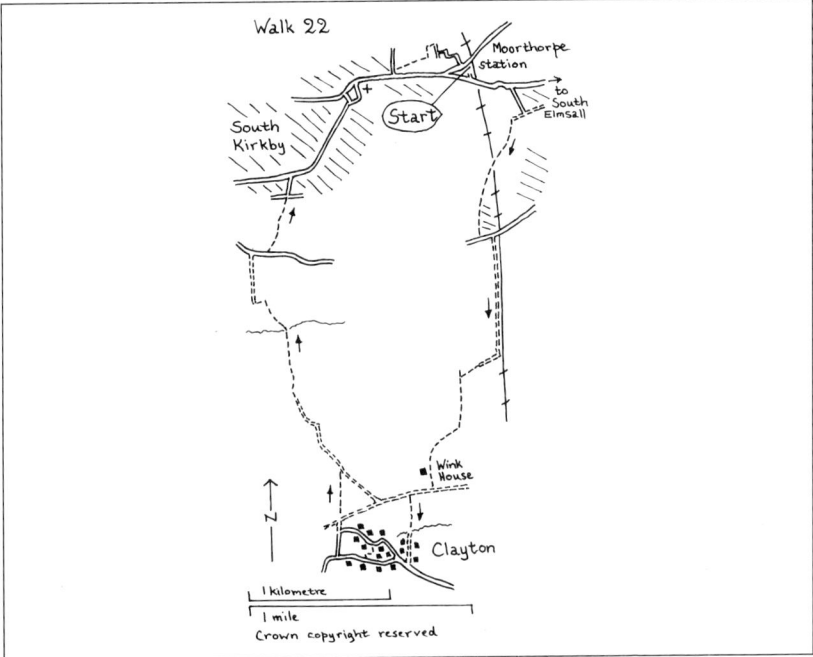

Walk 22

Moorthorpe Station

to South Elmsall

South Kirkby

Start

N

Wink House

Clayton

1 kilometre

1 mile

Crown copyright reserved

the left turn half left across the field towards the right hand corner of a hedge/wall (the boundary of a sports field). Pass the corner and bear left to the gap in the next cross hedge. Keep on the same line over the next field, pass through the fence into South Kirkby and cross the street to walk along a short ginnel. Continue forward up the next street.

At the next main road, Stockingate, turn right. As you approach the next main road, fork right. There is a small park with the War Memorial and a pond on the left. Pass to the right of the police station and turn left at the T-junction to pass South Kirkby's fine perpendicular limestone parish church. Turn right at the main road and cross it where convenient. On reaching The Green, cross the street which forks left and pass to the left of the public conveniences ahead to enter the park. Follow the path straight ahead, which soon climbs gently to pass the bowling green on the right and a football pitch on the left. Further along there are benches and picnic tables. At the far end turn left down the road, which soon turns right and reaches a car park. Leave it through the gate on the right, take the first street on the left, and at the next T-junction turn right. The road soon curves left and then right again to reach the main road. Cross the road and turn left for a few yards to the station entrance on the right.

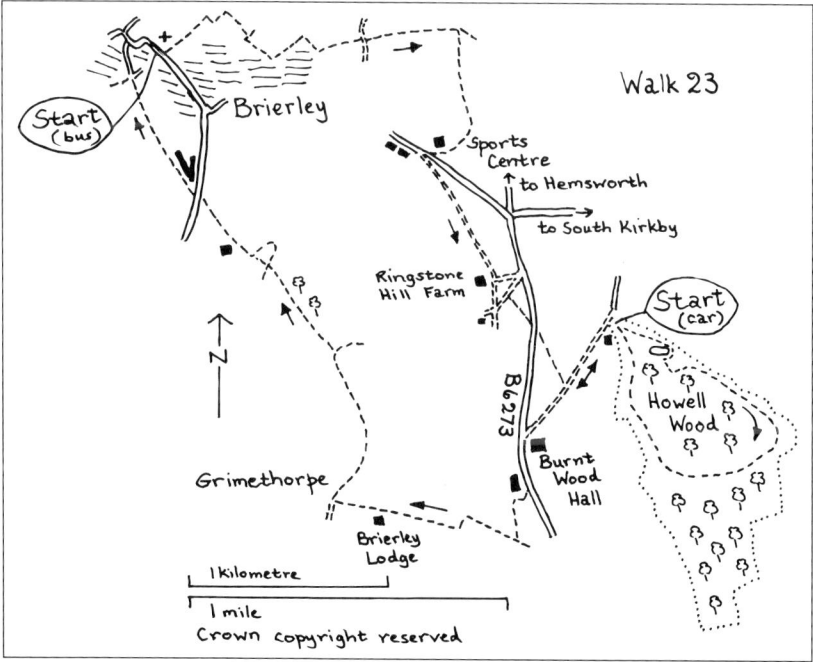

Walk 23

Crown copyright reserved

HOWELL WOOD COUNTRY PARK, GRIMETHORPE AND BRIERLEY
WALK 23

Full walk 7½ miles (12¼ km), circuit in the wood 1¾ miles (2¾ km); Pathfinder 716, 704. Most attractive undulating countryside with extensive views, almost entirely rural. Howell Wood was planted in the 1700s and contains a mix of trees, rhododendrons, a pond and ice-house and a picnic area. Most of this walk is in South Yorkshire, and one must compliment Barnsley MDC on the quality of their footpath signposting and waymarking.

By bus: Access to Howell Wood difficult. The easiest way is to take the 123 Wakefield-Grimethorpe bus to the Methodist Church on Church Street, Brierley and start the walk at [*].

By car: Howell Wood is signposted off Common Road, the road from Brierley to South Kirkby, about 600 yards east of the B6273 Hemsworth-Great Houghton road, down the access road to Avenue Farm, Burnt Wood Lane. Drive down the access road to the car park.

Firstly the walk around the country park. With your back to the car park entrance, take the left hand of the two paths leaving it into the wood. When you reach the pond, bear left round it. At the far end steps lead down left to the ice-house. Continue round the pond and take the first major path forking left uphill. At the junction at the top by a bench and a litter bin take the left hand of the two paths on the left, which leads back downhill. A few yards before you reach the beck at the bottom, bear right. The path leads down some steps, over a footbridge and up some steps, then down a few more steps and over another footbridge, parallel to the edge of the wood, but some way in.

When you are joined by a track from the right with the beck a yard or two to the left, keep forward. The path soon makes a right turn, still following the edge of the wood, before moving away from the edge, deeper into the wood. At a fork keep left, in a few yards crossing a footbridge and climbing three steps, and again keep left, to reach an open grassy strip. Bear right along this and follow it all the way to its end, where it widens and the path climbs to a bench and litter bin. This is the picnic area. There is a fine view back.

Keep forward for a few more yards and turn right along a cross track. You are now not far from the top edge of the wood. Having been joined by another track from the right, in a few yards fork left off the main track towards the edge of the wood. Follow this path, keeping always as close to the edge as possible, back to the car park.

Now for the rest of the walk. Leave the car park and turn left along Burnt Wood Lane. [#] Follow this track to the main road at Burnt Wood

Hall. There is a splendid view across the road to the west. Turn left along the road past the Hall, cross it, and immediately after passing Burnt Wood Cottages on the right, before the scrub starts, turn right along the signposted footpath. Follow the clear path through the wood until you reach a grassy open space where several paths meet, and turn right. When you reach a cross path at the bottom of the wood, turn left along it, but soon fork right into the large field. The path crosses straight over the field, aiming to the right hand end of the ruined buildings of Brierley Lodge, to a stile in the hedge 20 yards to the right of a gateway. Keep forward to join a track and follow it to the right of the buildings. From here there is a fine view right, and Grimethorpe lies spread out before you.

Follow the track down to the houses and turn right along the signposted bridleway, a track with a hedge to the left. Cross a stile by a metal barrier and continue with the hedge on your left for 60 yards, to find a path forking left through the hedge by an old concrete fence post. Take this path, with another hedge on the left and a small wood on the right. Soon the path is in a hollow way. When the bank on the right ends, cross the stile on the left by a metal barrier and walk along the right hand edge of the next field. Cross another metal barrier by a stile and keep forward with the fence/hedge on your right. When you reach a wood the path curves left. Pass through a stile on the right and walk along close to the bottom edge of the wood.

When the field on the left outside the wood ends, turn sharp left steeply down the slope, with the field still on your left, cross the footbridge and keep forward to reach a surfaced footpath. If you want you can continue straight up the facing grassy slope, but it is more pleasant to turn right along this path and follow it as it curves left and climbs gently to reach the top, passing benches with a fine view back over the way you have come. At the top, with the high boundary fence of a school ahead, turn right to a stile and walk straight across the field to pick up an old fence on the left. Follow this fence all the way to a stile leading out onto a road on the edge of Brierley. Cross diagonally left to the track opposite, but after a few yards on it fork right through a stile and follow the right hand edge of fields, with another splendid view left, until you join a paved path which leads to a kissing-gate in a corner.

Ignore the bridleway sign pointing left and take the left hand of the two streets on the right, which leads down to the main road in Brierley. Turn right past the post office, pass the little Dean-Hancock Garden with two benches, and when the road bends right ignore the footpath sign on the corner pointing left. Cross the road.

[*] Take the signposted bridleway to the right of Brierley Methodist Church. Having passed through the farm keep forward along the track. Now follow the directions closely, as we weave our way through the fields behind Brierley! The track turns right (ignore the footpath sign on the corner pointing left) then sharp left again, then right again, and when

it swings left again you leave it and take the footpath in the corner on the right. When it forks, keep left across waste ground to reach a cross path by a marker post. Turn left, with a ditch, hedge and football pitch to your right and another football pitch, then houses, to your left. When you reach a break in the houses on the left with a patch of grass, turn left and walk along the far side of this grass. The path is soon between fences. Pass through a barrier, cross a street, pass through the barrier opposite, and when you reach the field turn right along its right hand edge.

In the next corner turn left with the field edge, and when the hedge on the right ends and you reach a cross track keep straight forward across the middle of an enormous field. You reach the far side at a pylon. Ignore the path straight ahead and turn right to follow the track on the left hand side of the field boundary. At the top of the slope follow the wall on the right round to the right. It is followed by a fence/hedge. Pass a gate on the right into Burnt Wood Sports Centre, and again you have a wall on the right. Leave the track and keep with this wall, which leads to a stile. Cross the access road to the sports centre and follow the surfaced path opposite along to the road. Cross the road, walk along the left hand edge of the grass opposite, then turn sharp left along a track, soon with a field boundary on your right. Again there are extensive views to the right. Pass to the left of Ringstone Hill Farm, cross straight over the access road, and follow the track to the next cross track, where you turn left.

Walking along this track you pass a telegraph pole, and then another, and about 10 yards beyond this second one a path crosses the field on the right, not at a right angle to the track but slightly right of that. Follow this path to the main road, cross on the same line to the footpath sign opposite, then continue on the same line over the next field. At the far side drop down the bank and turn left along the track to return to the car park at Howell Wood. (If those who have come by bus want to do the circuit through the country park, they should turn left at this point, and on reaching the car park jump to the start of the walk description. If they want to omit the walk in the wood they should turn right and jump to [#] in the walk description.)

DID YOU KNOW that you can walk out of Leeds City Station, turn right and in a few minutes find yourself on a direct footpath route to the source of the River Aire, 50 miles away at Malham Tarn in the heart of the Yorkshire Dales?

Details of the whole route, which follows as far as possible riverside paths, are given in Douglas Cossar's *The Airedale Way.*

The book contains 16 circular and 2 linear rambles which cover the whole of Airedale from Malham Tarn to Castleford and include the entire towpath of the Leeds and Liverpool Canal between Leeds and Gargrave. Riverside paths and walks to notable viewpoints open up a variety of landscapes and a wealth of natural beauty, with old stone bridges, ancient churches, picturesque villages, historic farmhouses and many relics of the Industrial Revolution.

The Airedale Way is published by the West Riding Area of the RA at **£4.50** and is available from local booksellers, or direct from the publishers at 27 Cookridge Avenue, Leeds LS16 7NA price £5.30 including post & packing (cheques payable to Ramblers' Association please).

HEMSWORTH CIRCULAR
WALK 24

5¼ miles (9¼ km); Pathfinder 704. The route through Hemsworth itself is rather scruffy, but there is pleasant countryside around and the walk makes use of part of the fine new bridleway alongside the Hemsworth bypass.

By bus: 88 Pontefract-S.Kirkby, 198 Wakefield-S.Elmsall, 246 Pontefract-Barnsley, 249 Pontefract-Upton, 497/498 Wakefield-Doncaster to the stop just before the Hemsworth bypass. The walk starts at the car park beside the bypass.

By car: There is a new car park at the junction of the B6422 Hemsworth-S.Kirkby road and the Hemsworth bypass. Park here.

Leave the car park and turn left along the signposted bridleway, parallel to the bypass, which here follows the line of a former railway. Cross the B6273 at the South Moor Roundabout and continue along the fenced bridleway on the other side. Shortly before you reach the Brierley Roundabout you will see a public footpath signposted on both sides of the bypass. It crosses your bridleway, and when you reach it, turn right through the metal barrier and walk half right over the field, soon to join a track, along which you bear right. The views right are quite extensive. When you are under the power lines, ignore a track forking left to follow a hedge to the road, and further along ignore another track forking left to buildings.

On reaching Hemsworth, the track becomes a street: keep forward along it and follow it all the way to the next main road (Market Street). Cross this and turn right for a short distance, then take the first lane on the left, soon entering an enclosed footpath. At the end turn left along the street in Little Hemsworth, but on the next right hand bend enter a fenced footpath ahead, which follows the bend round for a few yards, but then you should fork left off it down another enclosed footpath. This soon turns left and then right again. Cross a street and continue up the ginnel. Climb some steps to reach Station Road and bear right along it.

Immediately after the Hemsworth Centre of Wakefield College turn right down the signposted footpath beside the college boundary fence. Cross a college access road. The path turns left, passes through dense blackberry bushes and turns right to cross the railway by a bridge. Go through a fence into a field and turn right along its edge. On reaching the rugby pitch turn left to pass behind the goalposts, then keep forward along the field boundary ahead. On reaching a small wood bear left through it, then bear right across the remainder of the field to a barrier in the wooden fence.

Cross the bypass to the continuation of the footpath and bear slightly left over the next field to Royd Moor Lane. Turn right along it.

Turn into the next access drive on the right to Royd Moor House. When the drive forks, cross the stile on the right of the right hand drive and walk along the edge of the field with the fence on your left. When the fence turns left, keep straight forward to a stile and then on along the left hand edge of the next field. Follow the field boundary when it turns left, and opposite the entrance to Royd Moor House Farm on the left turn right down the track. In 120 yards turn right along another track. Pass along the right hand edge of the narrow Bullinger Wood. After a while you join a better track and the bypass is once more in front of you.

Don't go through the tunnel under the bypass, but turn left along the signposted bridleway before it. The track soon bends left away from the road, parallel to the mainline railway down below on the right. Cross the railway by the next bridge, then follow the track on the right, which at first is parallel to the railway but then curves left towards the bypass and drops parallel to this and becomes fenced. Turn right to pass through the tunnel under the bypass, and then turn left along the fenced bridleway (curiously signposted here as a footpath!) and follow it back to your starting point.

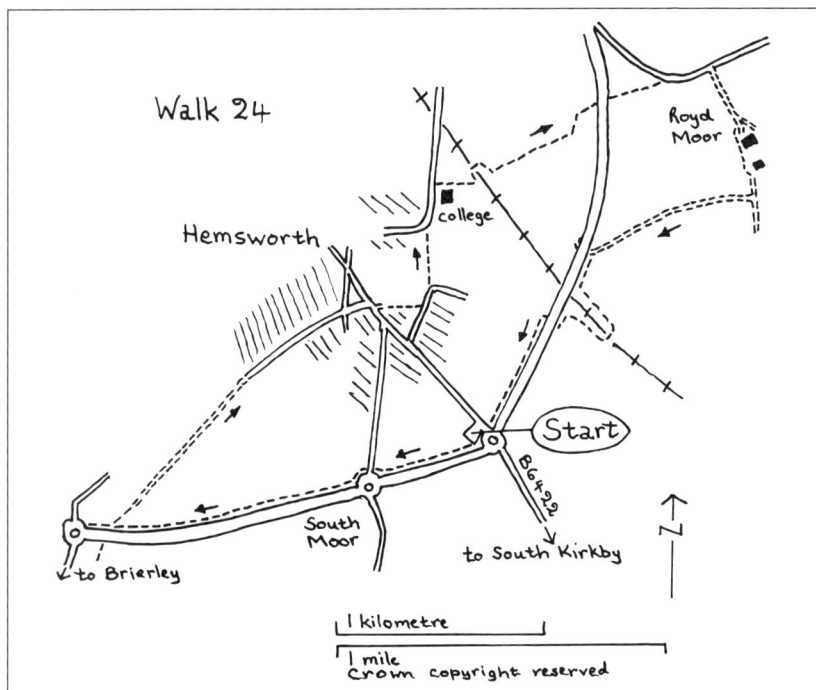

Walk 24

Hemsworth

college

Royd Moor

Start

South Moor

to South Kirkby

to Brierley

N →

1 kilometre

1 mile
Crown copyright reserved

HEMSWORTH TO HOWELL WOOD AND BRIERLEY
WALK 25

6½ miles (10½ km); Pathfinder 704, 716. A quiet, rural walk mainly on old tracks and taking in some reclaimed mine workings.

By bus: 88 Pontefract-South Kirkby, 198 Wakefield-South Elmsall, 246 Pontefract-Barnsley, 249 Pontefract-Upton, 497/498 Wakefield-Doncaster to the last stop before the roundabout on the new Hemsworth bypass (A628) on the road from Hemsworth to South Kirkby. Walk on towards the roundabout and turn left through a gate into a fenced bridleway.

By car: Car park on the junction of the B6422 Hemsworth-South Kirkby road and the new A628 Hemsworth bypass. Leave the car park and cross the B6422 and turn left for a few yards to go through a gate on the right into a fenced bridleway.

Follow the fenced bridleway until with the A628 ahead it turns left. Turn right here to leave the bridleway through a metal barrier. Turn right back towards the roundabout, but when you draw level with a large metal double gate on the other side of the road, cross over, go through it and turn left along a track, formerly a railway line. Having passed under power lines the path forks: keep right, between a wood on your left and a fence on your right. You are going to follow this fence for a considerable way, walking on reclaimed mine workings. After a time the mainline railway is over to the left, but you keep with the fence which curves right and for a time you have the valley of Hague Hall Beck on your left. Then the fence curves right again uphill, along the right hand edge of the wood.

With the buildings of Hague Hall Farm on the far side of the field ahead the fence turns sharp left. Follow it down. The wood ends and the beck is closeby on the left. Walk forward parallel to the beck, and as you approach a cross hedge bear slightly right to pass through the hedge and go down a few steps, then walk straight forward and cross a stile into a field. Continue forward along the left hand edge of the field, then turn right with the boundary in the next corner. Walk up the edge of this long field, and near the top corner cross a footbridge on the left. Turn right and follow the right hand edge of the field with the beck to your right. As you approach the road follow the field edge all the way round to the footpath signpost.

Cross the road diagonally right to the bridleway opposite, which keeps along to the right of a wall into an enclosed track. This is Hague Lane, an ancient route which one should be able to follow to Holmsley

Lane on the edge of South Kirkby, but unfortunately a section of it has been ploughed out, although the right to use it survives. So when the lane ends abruptly at a very large field, keep straight forward parallel to the beck away over to the right, and with luck you should gradually draw near to a hedge on the left, which you meet at an old stone gatepost near where this hedge turns sharp left. Bear right along this hedge and turn sharp left with it, then when the field boundary goes sharp right again, stay with it, but when you reach a group of taller trees on the left, where a hedge comes in from the left, about 100 yards from the wood in front, turn left through the trees, back into the delightful old enclosed way. Now it can be followed easily. It climbs gently and reaches a track. There are fine views to the left. Keep forward along the track until you reach the road, where you turn right (it is safer to cross to the other side, as there is no footway). At the next junction turn left along Common Road and follow it as far as the first lane on the right, Burnt Wood Lane, the access road to Avenue Farm and Howell Wood Country Park

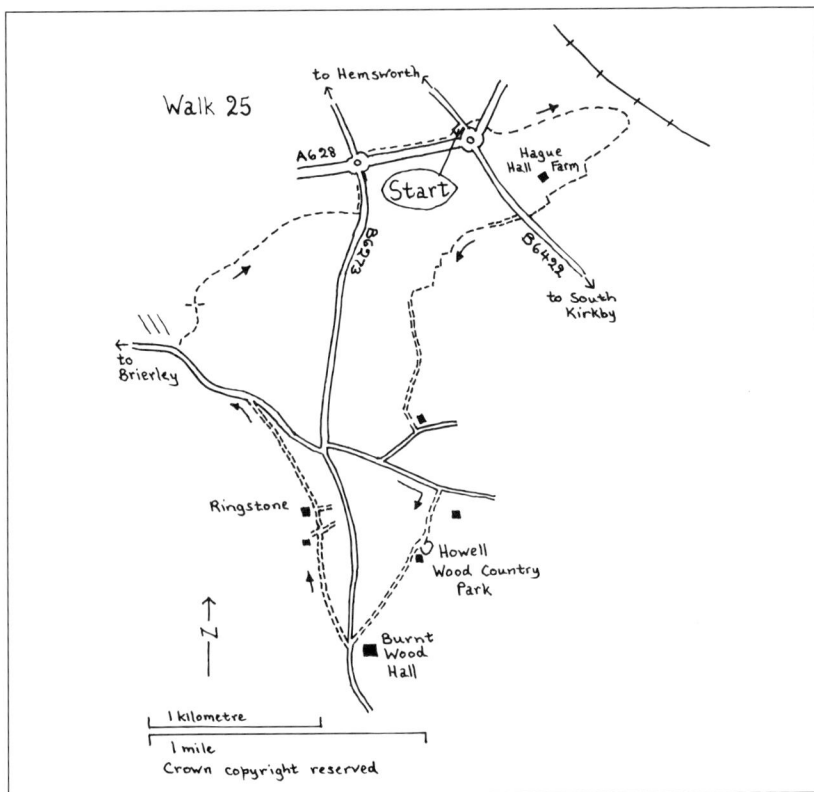

Walk 25

to Hemsworth

A628

Start

Hague Hall Farm

B6428

to South Kirkby

to Brierley

Ringstone

Howell Wood Country Park

N

Burnt Wood Hall

1 kilometre

1 mile

Crown copyright reserved

Follow this track past the Howell Wood Country Park car park and all the way to the B6273 at Burnt Wood Hall, cross the road (there is a fine view ahead), turn right and immediately take the track forking left and following the left hand edge of a field. Pass to the right of Ringstone Hill Farm, where you cross straight over two cross tracks, and continue with the field boundary on your left to Common Road on the outskirts of Brierley. Turn left along the footway and follow it until about 30 yards after the start of the 30 mph limit, where you cross the road and take the track opposite signposted to Hemsworth. Follow this track all the way over what used to be Hemsworth South Moor until you reach the B6273 again.

Turn left along the footway. A few yards before you reach South Moor Roundabout cross the road on your right, turn left and cross the A628, then turn left again for a few yards towards the roundabout and pass through a metal barrier in the fence on the right and turn right along the fenced bridleway, soon crossing over a farm access track. Follow the bridleway to the next road, the B6422, which was your starting point.

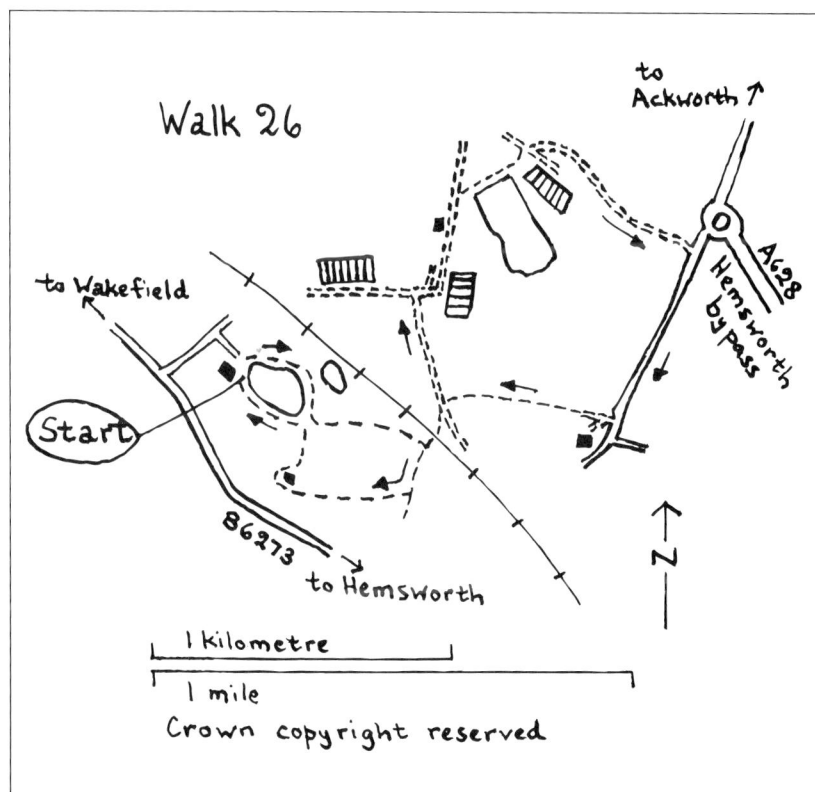

Walk 26

to Ackworth

to Wakefield

A628
Hemsworth bypass

Start

B6273

to Hemsworth

N

1 Kilometre

1 mile

Crown copyright reserved

HEMSWORTH WATER PARK AND
VALE HEAD PARK
WALK 26

3 miles (5 km); Pathfinder 704. An excellent family ramble, with lots of variety, the lakes, children's playgrounds, minigolf, and, as an added bonus, the turkey farms, although you won't see any turkeys! Some paths can be muddy after rain, when wellies would be advisable. An orienteering pack is available in the pub.

By bus: 123 Wakefield-Grimethorpe, 198 Wakefield-South Elmsall, 245 Pontefract-Barnsley, 497/498 Wakefield-Doncaster. The Water Park is signposted off the main road in Kinsley.

By car: the Water Park is signposted off the B6273 opposite the Farmers pub in Kinsley. Access is by Hoyle Mill Road: watch out for the right turn to the car park by the Windsurfer pub, toilets and lake.

From the car park/pub walk clockwise round the lake. At the first junction keep right, by the lake. With the smaller lake ahead, turn right at a T-junction over the bridge and keep right on the main path by the large lake. Cross another bridge and keep left at the fork, leaving the lake, cross another bridge - ahead is the children's play area - bear left and pass through bollards, then walk along the left hand edge of the golf course. Soon the path leads through woodland, with the golf course still nearby on the right. After a time you are walking parallel to the railway on the left. Turn left to pass under it. A few yards after the bridge keep left at a fork, and on reaching the concrete road, turn left along it.

When you reach a T-junction at Hemsworth Turkey Farms, turn right. Ignore the road left to the weighbridge, but a few yards further on bear left with the road. Having passed to the right of some bungalows and the fishermen's car park, fork right off the road to cross a footbridge and keep forward along the embankment of Hoyle Mill Dam. On the far side cross another footbridge and continue into the field, then bear slightly left across it to a stile on the far side. Turn right along the road, in a few yards forking left along an unsurfaced track, with Hoyle Mill Turkey Farm straight ahead. At the end of a narrow wood on the right ignore a track forking right and keep forward up over the middle of the field, enjoying the fine open views, to reach the main road.

Turn right along the footway. Pass Hagg Wood and at the far end turn right down the access road to Marsh Farm. Immediately the road forks left to the farm, but our route lies straight forward along a grassy track.

Cross a stile into a field and walk down it following exactly the overhead power lines. Leave the field over another stile, cross a plank bridge and walk forward, bearing slightly left into the adjacent field, then walk along the right hand edge of this to another stile. Cross the concrete road and follow the path opposite, which should be familiar to you.

Pass under the railway again, but now keep forward up the left hand edge of the golf course. After a time the path acquires a macadam surface. At a fork keep left uphill past several benches. We are now in Vale Head Park. The view is excellent. At the next fork again keep left, and at the fork by the shelter again keep left. The path now descends and curves right. At the next fork again keep left, and at the next one again go left, over a small stone bridge, then bear left up through the rose garden. Pass to the left of the clubhouse then immediately turn right to another nice view. Ahead is the children's play area.

Walk down the slope, with minigolf on the left, then pass to the right of the children's playground, go between a shelter and a small pond and keep descending, soon with a beck beside you on the right. At the far end of the play area go left past the bollard and walk forward to the lake. Bear left round it, and choosing always the path which keeps as close as possible to it, return to your starting point.

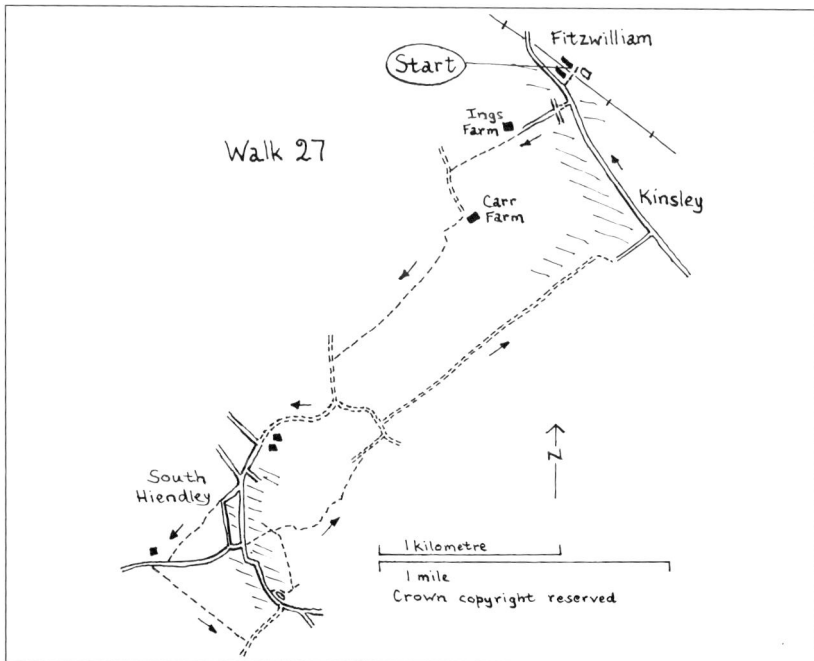

Walk 27

Start

Fitzwilliam

Ings Farm

Carr Farm

Kinsley

South Hiendley

1 kilometre

1 mile

Crown copyright reserved

73

FITZWILLIAM TO SOUTH HIENDLEY
WALK 27

5½ miles (9 km); Pathfinder 704, 703. A pleasant stroll through gently undulating arable countryside.

By train: the walk starts and finishes at Fitzwilliam Station

By car: there is a large free car park at Fitzwilliam Station.

If coming from Wakefield by train, or if parked in the car park, cross the railway line by the footbridge and walk down the ginnel to the main road. Cross it and turn left, and in 100 yards turn right along a track just before the filling station. When the track ends, keep straight forward along Farm Lane. When the surface ends, keep forward along the track, which passes to the left of Ings Farm, then follow the left hand edge of the following field. On reaching a farm track, turn left, and when you arrive at the buildings of Carr Farm turn right at the footpath sign along the left hand edge of a field. At the end of the field kink left and right and continue on the same line as before, with a hedge on your right.

Pass under the power lines and at the next field corner ignore a footbridge on the right and turn left along the field boundary. After about 100 yards there is a rusty footpath sign on the right and a wide gateway with wooden gateposts. Turn right through this and walk straight up the large field (the line of the path should be clear), heading for the left hand end of a strip of woodland at the top. Walk straight forward to the left of this into the next field, then straight across this (in the direction of the right hand end of a collection of farm buildings on the skyline). On the far side of the field turn left up the old hedged track, Cross Hill Lane. It swings to the right and is joined by another track from the left. Keep on to Upper Hiendley Farm, where the track becomes surfaced. Follow it to the junction with a road, and keep forward into South Hiendley.

On reaching the main road, cross diagonally left to follow Tun Lane opposite. When the lane swings left, keep forward along the fenced footpath. Cross a tiny footbridge and walk forward along the left hand edge of the following field. Keep this line to the next road and turn right along the footway for 60 yards to a signposted path on the left. It leads to a stile which you cross, ignoring a clear path which bears left along the fence, then walk up the left hand edge of the field. Cross the stile in the next corner and, ignoring a stile on the left, keep forward with the fence on your left. Cross the stile in the bottom corner of this field and keep forward along the track.

On reaching the main road at the southern end of South Hiendley, cross it and turn left. Having passed the duckpond over the wall on the right, turn right along a track - there is a pleasant bench here - but soon fork right off it to cross a small clapper bridge. A few yards further on fork left, and in another 40 yards fork left again, keeping the beck down on your left. A path joins you from the right and you cross a concrete bridge. Pass a redundant stile and walk along the left hand edge of the following field. At the far end fork left and drop to another redundant stile, then follow a wooden fence on the right to yet another redundant stile and turn right along the track.

When the hedge on the right ends, ignore a track forking right and keep forward with a hedge on the left, and when the main track turns left through this hedge, keep forward along a less clear track, still with the hedge to your left. The hedge becomes intermittent and finally ends by an old stone gatepost. Keep straight forward across the middle of the large field, at an angle of about 30° to the field boundary on the right. Over the brow of the hill you head for a solitary tree on the far side of the field, and when you reach it turn right along the track. At the next junction of tracks turn left, and in another 100 yards at the next junction turn right. Follow this track all the way to Kinsley.

On reaching the houses, cross the concrete barrier over the track and keep forward to the right of the houses. Follow the track to the end, and where the high fence on the right bends right, cross diagonally over the patch of grass and at the far corner bear right along a footpath. At the next cross track turn left and walk straight forward along the street to the main road. Turn left here for the last ½-mile back to your starting point.

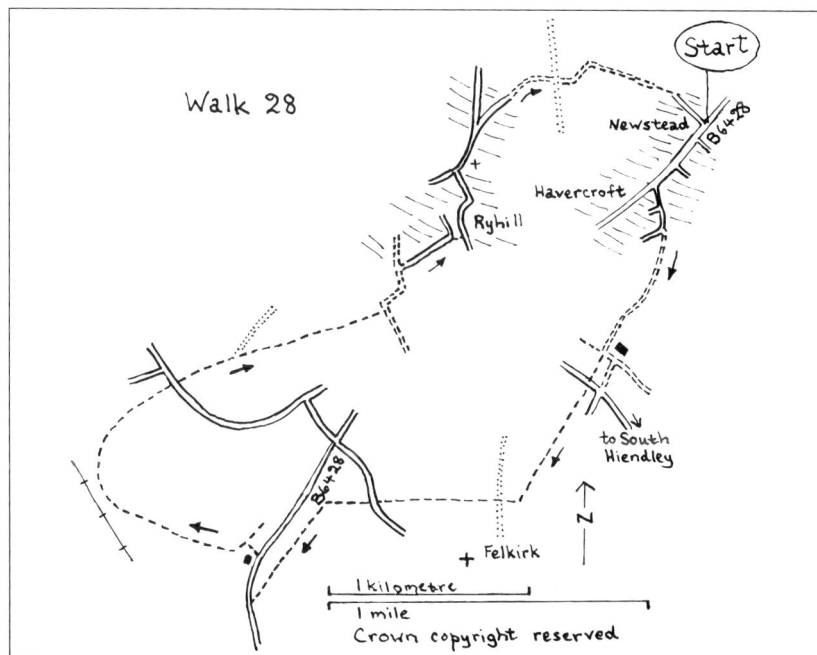

Walk 28

Start

Newstead

Havercroft

Ryhill

to South Hiendley

Felkirk

N

1 kilometre

1 mile

Crown copyright reserved

RYHILL CIRCULAR
WALK 28

5¾ miles (9¼ km); Pathfinder 703. A ramble of considerable variety, using old tracks, disused railways and a path through reclaimed mine workings. Pleasant views.

By bus: No. 196 Wakefield-Newstead to the last stop on Newstead Lane. No. 295 Pontefract-South Elmsall, 339/342 Barnsley-Hemsworth could be taken to Ryhill and the walk joined at [*].

By car: Park considerately in Upper Hatfield Place, which is the last street on the left off Newstead Lane in Newstead when driving towards Fitzwilliam, immediately before the end of the 30 mph limit. Walk back to Newstead Lane and turn right along it.

Walk down Newstead Lane into Havercroft, cross the beck in the dip and just after the bus shelter turn left along East Street. Where this turns right as South Street, keep forward along a narrow tarmac lane, passing round a large gate, and at once you are among fields. Follow this old road (Tup Lane) until it turns left through double gates (a footpath comes in from the right): here leave it and keep forward along another footpath. Cross over the next road (Brier Lane) and continue along the footpath opposite, on the bed of a former tramway. After a time Felkirk Church comes into view ahead. Having crossed a small brick bridge the track bends right and crosses the trackbed of another old railway. The church is now over to the left.

When you reach the next road, cross straight over and continue on the old tramway to the next road. Turn right along this, pass a bungalow and cross a footbridge on the left to follow a path up to a fence. Turn left along this and follow it along reclaimed mine workings, with woodland on the left and fields on the right. After the fence curves right, there are extensive views left. The path drops and levels out, then curves right again. With a wood immediately ahead the path bears left away from the fence. There are railway lines down below on the left, but the path, running through woodland, soon bears away from them again. Cross straight over a narrow cross path, pass between two concrete blocks and bear right along a cross track, passing between more concrete blocks.

Cross straight over the next road to follow the footpath opposite. When you reach an embankment on the left it would be possible to climb the path which zigzags up it and follow the old railway line to Ryhill, but I suggest you continue straight ahead along the pleasant tree-lined path. On reaching a cross track, turn left, then in a few yards follow the track right and a short distance further on left again. In about 80 yards at a crossing of tracks turn right again, and then keep forward along the following street into Ryhill. When the street turns left, keep forward down the steps to reach the main road opposite the post office. Turn left.

The main road curves left. [*] At the next junction ignore Station Road on the left and follow the main road right (Nostell Lane). Pass the parish church and 150 yards further on fork right along Common Ing Lane. Follow this to the end and keep forward down the footpath. When you reach a junction of paths and tracks, cross straight over the bed of the disused railway and take the track opposite. When you reach a fork, follow the main track left, but in a few yards fork right off it along a narrow footpath with a hedge on the right. Pass through the kissing-gate at the end and keep forward along the street, which is Upper Hatfield Place.

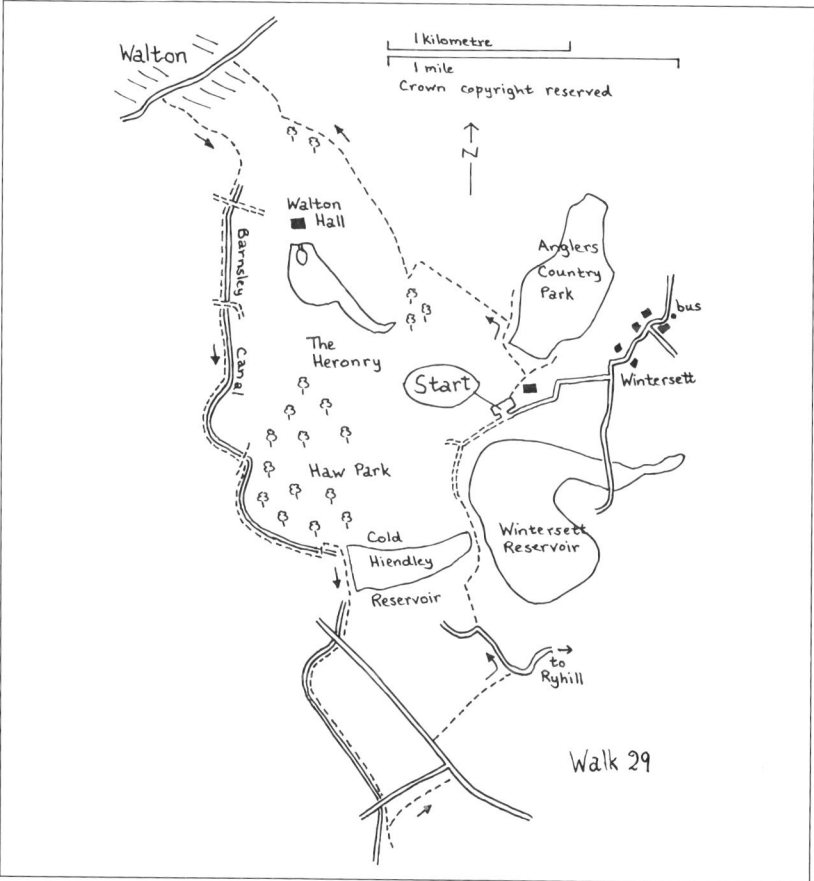

Walton

1 kilometre
1 mile
Crown copyright reserved

↑
N

Walton Hall

Barnsley Canal

Anglers Country Park

bus

The Heronry

Start

Wintersett

Haw Park

Wintersett Reservoir

Cold Hiendley Reservoir

→ to Ryhill

Walk 29

WALTON PARK AND THE HERONRY
WALK 29

7 miles (11½ km); Pathfinder 703. The Heronry is a large area of countryside which includes the Walton Hall estate, Haw Park Wood, Anglers Country Park and Wintersett and Cold Hiendley Reservoirs. It can be explored with the help of two leaflets produced by Wakefield Countryside Service, *Discover the Heronry* and *The Waterton Trail, four easy to follow walks around the Heronry.* The present walk follows the boundary of the Walton Hall estate and a long section of towpath of the disused Barnsley Canal. The area is of great interest to birdwatchers.

By bus: 195, 196 Wakefield-Newstead/South Hiendley/Hemsworth to Wintersett; continue on foot through the village, and after leaving it take the first minor road on the right, Haw Park Lane, signposted to Anglers Country Park and follow it to the main car park.

By car: Anglers Country Park and the Waterton Countryside Discovery Centre are well signposted from surrounding roads. The car park is on Haw Park Lane (GR 375 153).

From the Waterton Countryside Discovery Centre, opened in 1995 and named after Charles Waterton (1782-1865), a naturalist who lived at Walton Hall, follow the tarmac path towards the lakes. Waymarks indicate the Waterton Trail. On approaching the large lake, keep left at the fork, and soon you reach the lake. Shortly a path on the left gives access to a hide, and a little further on a track through a gate leads to another hide with a view over the large lake. Having returned to the main track, look out for a signposted stile on the left. Cross it and in 10 yards go through a large gate on the left and turn right along the track. When the track leads through a gate on the right, keep forward along the fence to the next stile, then on by the fence to the bottom of the next field, where you cross a stile and footbridge and follow the fenced path left.

On reaching the boundary wall of the Walton Hall estate, turn sharp right. Now you must follow this wall, crossing several stiles on the way, until it turns sharp left and the houses of Walton are before you. Here leave the wall and keep forward with a fence to your right. After you cross the brow of the hill and the fence begins to curve right, bear half left across the large field to a stile near the far left hand corner. Cross this and turn left along the road through Walton.

Turn left along the signposted footpath opposite Walton Sports and Social Club. Ignore paths forking left and right, and having left the houses of Walton you once more reach the familiar boundary wall of Walton

Hall. After a time the former Barnsley Canal is between you and the wall. You will now follow the towpath for a considerable distance. Pass the golf course clubhouse and walk under a stone bridge over the canal. Ignore a clear path forking right. The canal passes through a deep cutting and you walk under another high stone bridge. As you enter the wood, the canal is crossed by a wooden bridge, Clay Royd Bridge, which carries a public bridleway. Ascend the steps to the right of the bridge and descend the steps on the other side to continue along the towpath.

Cross the next bridge, another stone one, and immediately turn right down some steps and continue by the canal. On reaching a crossing of paths turn right, back across the canal on a footbridge to a gap-stile. To shorten the walk turn left here on a path between Cold Hiendley Reservoir on the right and a drainage channel on the left and follow it until you reach a cross track with the embankment of Wintersett Reservoir ahead. Climb the embankment and turn left, then jump to [#] below. For the full walk keep forward over another footbridge and walk along the track with the reservoir to your left. At the far end of the embankment cross another bridge and bear right along the track, with the canal once more on your right. Just before you reach the next motor road, fork right on a narrow footpath which cuts the corner and brings you out onto the road by Cold Hiendley Bridge.

Cross the road and follow the path opposite, again the canal towpath. After a time the canal passes through a deep cutting and you reach High Bridge. Pass under this, but after another 200 yards the path climbs some steps and leads away from the canal. On reaching a cross path, with some stone bollards to the right, turn left and follow this path, the track of an old railway line, to the next road, reached at a barrier. Cross the road and turn left along it for about 250 yards, then take the signposted bridleway on the right and follow it across a very large field. At the next road turn left. Where the road bends left at Cold Hiendley, ignore the first footpath sign on the right, but follow the second one, a few yards before the start of the 30 mph limit, onto a clear path straight across the field.

After a time you are walking to the right of a mass of blackberries, and soon the path swings right across the middle of the field, with Cold Hiendley Reservoir down to your left. Go through the hedge on the far side and turn left along a cross path. Wintersett Reservoir is to your right. Cross the embankment between the two reservoirs, both built last century to supply water to the Barnsley Canal. [#] A few yards before a metal footbridge drop left to join a track and turn right along it. On reaching a junction with a large metal gate on the left, turn right to return to your starting point.

ANGLERS COUNTRY PARK, CROFTON, SHARLSTON AND RYHILL
WALK 30

7¼ miles (11¾ km); Pathfinder 703. A country park, spacious arable countryside and a view of Nostell Priory.

By bus: 195/196 to the Royal Oak pub in Crofton. Walk back along the main street in the Wakefield direction and start the walk description at [#].

By car: Anglers Country Park and the Waterton Countryside Discovery Centre are well signposted from surrounding roads. The car park is on Haw Park Lane (GR 375 153). From the car park cross to the Discovery Centre and then take the track going anti-clockwise round the large lake.

Follow the track round the lake to the far end, where it is crossed by a fence and there is a junction of tracks. Turn right off the track and follow a wooden fence along to a stile. Cross the track beyond and walk down the edge of the field opposite with the fence/hedge on your right. Cross the stile at the bottom and walk up the next field with the fence/hedge on your left. At the top ignore a track on the left to Hare Park Farm, cross the stile and keep on along the field edge. As you cross the brow of the hill look half left to see the Wakefield skyline. Pass through the kissing-gate and turn right over the railway bridge, and follow the lane up to Crofton, crossing another former railway bridge on the way. At the main road turn left. Bus travellers can catch their return bus here.

[#] Near the top of the hill down out of the village turn right up a street to Crofton Parish Church, passing the old stocks on the right. Pass to the right of the church, keep right at a fork with a bench on the left and walk straight down through the churchyard into a ginnel. Drop to cross a footbridge and rise to join a street. Keep forward up the street and cross over another one into the continuation of the ginnel. At the next street turn left. Pass the Weavers Green pub and walk down to meet the A638. Cross with great care and turn right for a yard or two to where two public footpaths are signposted on the left.

Follow the one to the right, which crosses diagonally over the field aiming for a wooden pylon near the far hedge. The path bears left before you reach the pylon, crosses a ditch and continues towards the next field, but before reaching it turns right along the left hand edge of the field you are in, passing between the pylon and the hedge. Follow this headland path to the next road, cross it (to the left is the White Horse pub), ignore the road straight ahead and turn right for about 100 yards to a signposted path on the left. Walk up the fenced section, cross the stile and bear left then right to follow the boundary fence of the field, soon joining a track. Walk straight through the farmyard and keep on along the track, soon keeping right when it forks.

At the end of a section of redbrick wall on the left you reach a narrow ginnel on the left, which is worth following for a look at the charming

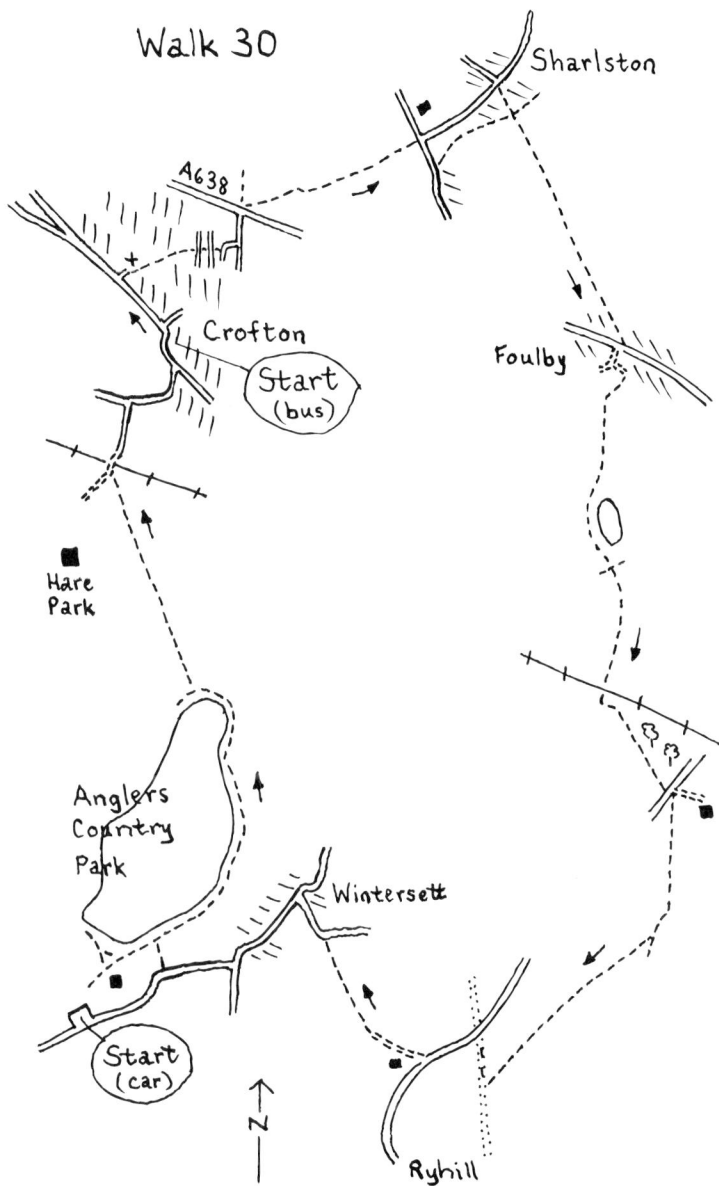

Walk 30

Sharlston

A638

Crofton

Start
(bus)

Foulby

Hare
Park

Anglers
Country
Park

Wintersett

Start
(car)

N ↑

Ryhill

1 kilometre

1 mile

Crown copyright reserved

village green in Sharlston. But to continue the walk turn right and follow a clear path with a hedge on your right. Follow the right hand edge of this field and the next one. The path leads into an enclosed footpath on the right which passes between houses to reach the A638 in Foulby. Cross the road and turn left, but take the first track on the right. In 50 yards keep left at the fork, but when the track bends left to the houses, keep straight forward on a path which bears right to a metal barrier and kissing-gate. Keep forward on a new track over reclaimed colliery land. As the track climbs and bears left, look left for a view to Nostell Priory.

Cross over a drainage ditch and a cross track and pass to the right of a new lake. At the far end cross straight over a cross track and soon you will see that you are heading towards a railway line. Pass under this and in 10 yards take the footpath on the left, which soon runs along the left hand edge of a field with Horncastle Wood to the left. The right of way continues up the field edge to the road, but most walkers fork left into the wood. If you do this, choose always the path closest to the right hand edge of the wood, particularly towards the far end, and when you are a few yards from the road bend right into the field and rejoin the right of way.

Cross the road to take the access road to Horncastle Farm, but at once fork right off it up a concrete track. When the track turns left to the water tower, keep straight forward to the corner of a wood then keep your line over the next field towards a hedge corner on the far side. A few yards to the right of this corner cross the ditch ahead and follow the left hand edge of the next field and the one after to its end, then immediately bear half right over the next large field to the hedge on the far side. Looking beyond this hedge, on the top of the rise there is a solitary tree: head for this. Cross through the hedge (there is a marker post) and walk up the middle of the next field to pass to the right of the tree and follow the field boundary on your left until it turns sharp left, then bear very slightly left over the next field, away from the field boundary on your right, to the next marker post in the far hedge. Walk straight on over the middle of the next field to the next marker post, then keep the same line across the next field to the far boundary, then forward to reach the trackbed of a disused railway.

Turn right along it and follow it to the next road (you can cut the corner). Turn left along the roadside verge, but when the road begins to curve left cross it and take a track down to the right of farm buildings. Pass through the remains of a railway bridge and the track narrows to a footpath. Follow it to the next road, then keep forward to Wintersett. At the T-junction turn left through the hamlet, and keep going until you reach a minor road on the right signposted to Anglers Country Park (Haw Park Lane). Follow it for about 250 yards to a signposted footpath on the right, where a stile leads into the country park. Keep forward at first, close to the right hand boundary, but the path soon bears left to the lake. Motorists will turn left here to return to the car park, bus walkers will turn right on the track round the lake and jump to the start of the walk description.

NOTTON
WALK 31

5 miles (8 km); Pathfinder 703. An attractive stroll through pleasant countryside with fine views, using two former railway lines. There is at present one short steep climb up a slippery bank on an unofficial path, but Wakefield Council intend to create a proper path.

By bus: 445, 446 Leeds-Wakefield-Barnsley, 449 Wakefield-Barnsley to Notton village green.

By car: Park in the large car park by the village hall on Notton green.

Leave the car park and with the village green in front of you turn right. Turn right into Ingswell Drive and when the road forks, keep right down Ingswell Avenue, but take the signposted path on the left after the first house. Follow the path forward with houses to the left and a field to the right, cross the footbridge at the end and turn right along the track. Follow this until you cross a disused railway line in a deep cutting. Turn right, then in 100 yards fork right down onto this railway line and turn left along it. On approaching a bridge carrying a road over the railway, fork left along a narrower path which leads under the bridge. Climb to a fence corner and keep forward between this fence and a hedge on the right.

Soon you drop again onto the trackbed of the old railway. Pass under the next bridge and after a time you come close to a railway line which still operates. Soon you approach the next high stone bridge. About 80 yards before it look for a path forking right and climbing very steeply up the bank. At the top bear left to join the road by the bridge. Cross the road to a barrier opposite and follow the clear path forward. Keep alongside the fence on the left for about 150 yards, then fork right along a path which keeps to the left hand edge of the field with a hedge to the left. Cross the bridge on the left over another old railway line and walk across the middle of the next field for about 50 yards until you reach a strip of rough ground, the end of another old railway line. Turn right along this strip. Soon you have a choice of paths.

On reaching a fork about 150 yards before houses, keep left and drop to join a road on the edge of Royston. Cross the main road and turn sharp right. Here a bridge used to carry the railway over the road. Immediately after its remains take the signposted bridleway on the left. This attractive path leads in time to a T-junction: turn left on the track to Applehaigh Farm. Pass to the right of all the buildings, cross a stile and keep forward. In 80 yards when the path forks keep right, then look out for a footbridge over the beck on the right. Over it turn left, following the beck at first, but soon the path climbs away from it and bears right to a stile. Walk up the hollow way, then pass into the field on the left and walk up its right hand edge as far as a marker post. Here fork half left across the field to a hedge corner visible on the far side, then keep forward with the hedge to your left. Cross a stile and continue with the hedge on your left. Follow the track straight up through the farmyard and turn right along the road to return to Notton.

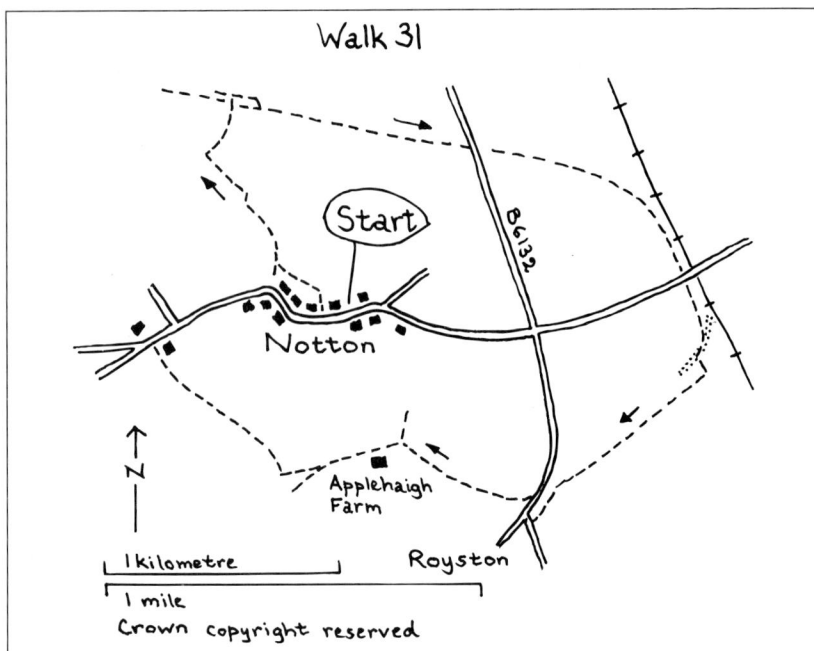

Walk 31

Start

B6132

Notton

N

Applehaigh
Farm

Royston

1 kilometre

1 mile

Crown copyright reserved

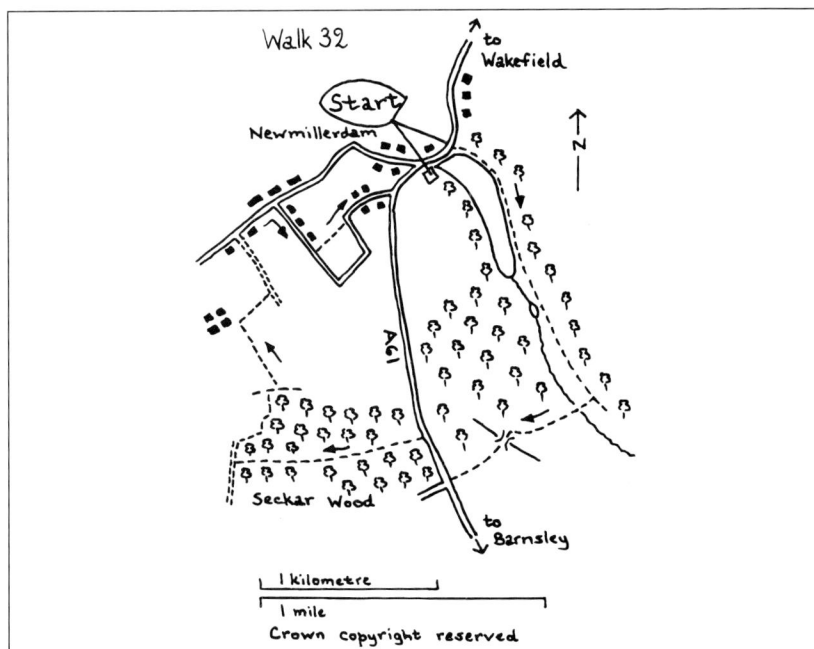

Walk 32

Start

to
Wakefield

Newmillerdam

N

A61

Seckar Wood

to
Barnsley

1 kilometre

1 mile

Crown copyright reserved

NEWMILLERDAM AND SECKAR WOOD
WALK 32

5 miles (8 km); Pathfinder 703. The walk follows the lakeside, passes through woods and heathland, and has good views of the city of Wakefield. Newmillerdam Country Park lies on the A61 Wakefield to Barnsley road. There are a number of cafés and pubs near the dam.

By bus: No. _445/446 Leeds-Wakefield-Barnsley, 449 Wakefield-Barnsley._

By car: Park either by the War Memorial near the Dam Inn (free, but limited) or in the large car park at the western end of the dam, opposite the Fox & Hounds (pay-and-display). Coming from Wakefield, if you fork right up School Hill, there is another free car park on the left.

Go through the iron gates by the War Memorial, into the grounds now owned by Wakefield District Council. Keep along the lake to its end, passing the old boat house (the first cornmill was probably built near here in 1285), the causeway across the lake and the walkway across the head of the lake, then swing right with the main path across a bridge over the feeder beck. You are faced by a T-junction: take neither the track to the right nor to the left, but cross over and bear slightly left up the slope through the trees. In a few yards bear right in front of a bench, still going gently uphill. Turn left along the first crossing path and on reaching a woodland drive go straight across, walking gently uphill to reach a clearing. Go through the clearing and on the far side bear right across a bridge over the old railway track. Follow the path forward with a high wire fence to the right to the main road.

Cross the main road with care and turn right along the pavement for about 300 yards. Turn left round a barrier across an old stone gateway on a track through Seckar Woods. Walk along the main track, keeping a close lookout for a ruined building in the trees about 15 yards to the left of it. A few yards further on you reach a clearing where you bear slightly left. Follow the track at first gently then rather more steeply uphill. At the heather keep on the track and continue uphill. Here the view opens out. Turn round to admire it. In front of you is Wakefield with its cathedral spire, with the prominent spire of Ossett Parish Church away to the left. Woolley village is to the right.

Continue along the heathland track until an old lane is reached by a stone gateway with a wooden barrier. Turn right; and when the lane ends go straight forward down the right hand edge of the field, keeping the wood to your right. When the fence turns right, go right with it. The mound of Sandal Castle can now be seen to the left of the power station.

Follow the the edge of the field until it turns sharp left and there is a wooden stile on the right. Cross this and in a yard or two turn left, ignoring the path straight on into the wood, cross a ditch by a bridge, and turn right along the edge of the field. Pass through the hedge in the field corner and cross a sleeper bridge, then turn left, keeping the hedge on your left.

Where the fence and hedge turn right near houses, go right with them, and when you reach a gap in the hedge on the left with a track going through it, turn left along the track and follow it all the way down to the road, which you reach by an old stone step-stile. Turn right along the road and pass several old stone cottages (one dated 1764). Pass Church Lane on the left and turn right into Wood Lane (bus stop for Wakefield and Leeds a few yards further on on the other side of the road). About 100 yards after passing the Pennine Camphill Community Centre turn left down a tarmac path between the fields to join a lane at a bend. Go straight forward down the lane (Almshouse Lane) to the main road (from which monarch's reign does the pillar-box on the corner date?). Turn left to return to your starting point. The Wheelhouse on the dam was once a cornmill, built in 1653 and in use until 1960: go down and have a look at the old waterwheel.

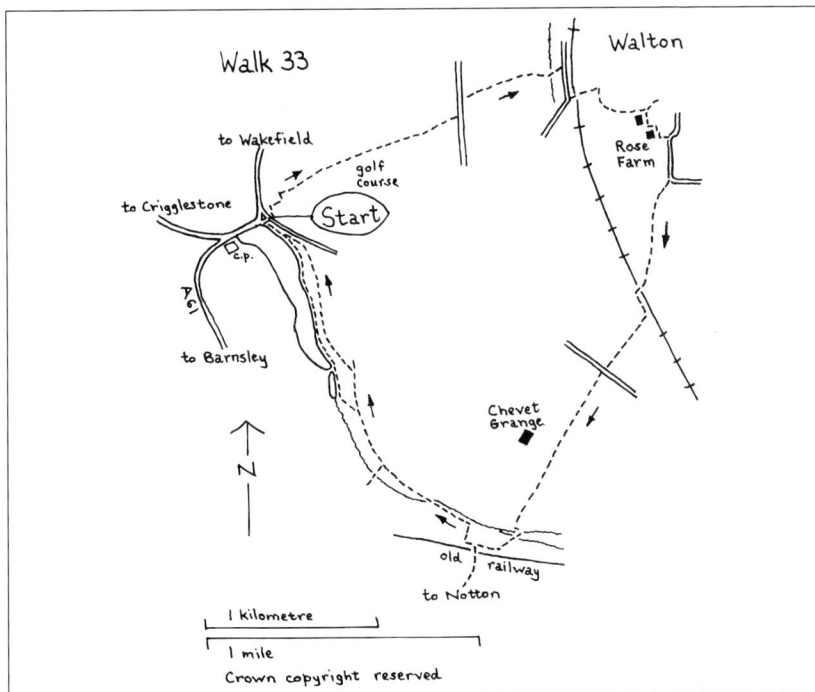

Walk 33

Walton

to Wakefield

to Crigglestone

golf course

Start

c.p.

to Barnsley

Rose Farm

N

Chevet Grange

old railway

to Notton

1 kilometre

1 mile

Crown copyright reserved

NEWMILLERDAM AND CHEVET
WALK 33

5 miles (8 km); Pathfinder 703. Country park; field paths and tracks. Newmillerdam Country Park lies on the A61 Wakefield to Barnsley road. There are a number of cafés and pubs near the dam.

By bus: No. 445/446 Leeds-Wakefield-Barnsley, 449 Wakefield-Barnsley.

By car: Park either by the War Memorial near the Dam Inn (free, but limited) or in the large car park at the western end of the dam, opposite the Fox & Hounds (pay and display). Coming from Wakefield, if you fork right up School Hill, there is another free car park on the left.

From the War Memorial walk up Hill Road. Near the top of the hill go up a few steps by the last house on the left, cross the road and follow the rough lane. In 50 yards turn right up a tarmac drive which soon becomes a path. Keep on this path, ignoring side paths to left or right, until you reach a stile leading on to a golf course. Follow a faint path in a dead straight line across several fairways (beware of flying golf balls!) to the far side of the golf course. The path continues in the same direction across another field to a road.

Turn left along the road for 100 yards to a gateway on the right and follow the path across a very large field, passing an old stone gatepost, to a pair of old gateposts in the hedge. Walk straight down the next field to a footbridge over the beck, and up the other side to a gap-stile and the road. Turn right. A footbridge over the railway on the left is reached by a step-stile in the wall by the hedge. Over a stile, continue up the edge of the field. At the top of the field turn right along the bottom edge of the wood and follow it round over two stiles. Now walk straight ahead towards the lefthand end of a modern barn, but then bear left to the stile by the gate. Turn right along the track for a yard or two to a stile on the left. Now turn right down the side of the farm buildings to another stile. Turn left along the track which curves right and left past the nicely restored Rose Farm.

At the road turn right, and at the top of the hill, where the road turns left (signposted to Wintersett and Cold Hiendley) keep straight on along the hedged track. Where the track bears left into the next field, keep straight forward along a footpath, with the old hedge to the left. Where this old field boundary turns sharp left, keep forward over the field to a fence. Here a fenced path leads down left to a footbridge over the railway. Climb left up the other side and turn left down the field edge. At the corner of the field turn right along the hedge, in a few yards cross a stile, and follow the left hand edge of the field to a stile in the far corner. Keep the hedge on your left along the next field, cross a stile in the corner and continue in the same direction with the hedge on your left to the road.

Cross the road to a signposted footpath a yard or two to the right and then walk straight across the enormous field, aiming for a solitary tree in the distance. You will pass the end of a wall coming from Chevet Grange Farm on the right, then the tree, and soon you will be following a wall on your right. At the foot of the field go left for a few yards to find an old stone bridge over Bleakley Dike. Turn right alongside the Dike, cross a beck by a bridge, and bear left straight up across the field towards a large concrete post. Turn right along the track for 200 yards to find a clear path on the right which drops back down across the field to the beck. Turn left along the beck until you reach a footbridge over it. Cross this and turn left along the edge of the field until you come to a path bearing right across the field to the edge of the wood. This is another entrance to Newmillerdam Country Park. You might wish to explore it in more detail.

But to return to your starting point keep straight along the path, ignoring other paths to right and left. You will reach a prominent fork. By going left you would drop to the side of the lake, which could be followed all the way back, but the more interesting (and quieter) route is to keep right on the higher path. Just before this path leads you out of the wood through an old gateway fork half left off it on a narrower, descending path with pleasant views down to the lake. Shortly after passing an old quarry on the right, keep forward on the left hand of the paths, which soon takes you down a long flight of steps. Just after these there is a chance to turn left down a broad path to the lakeside, but again it is pleasanter to keep forward along the narrower path, which continues to lead through the woods and brings you down to the lakeside just before the main entrance to the Park.

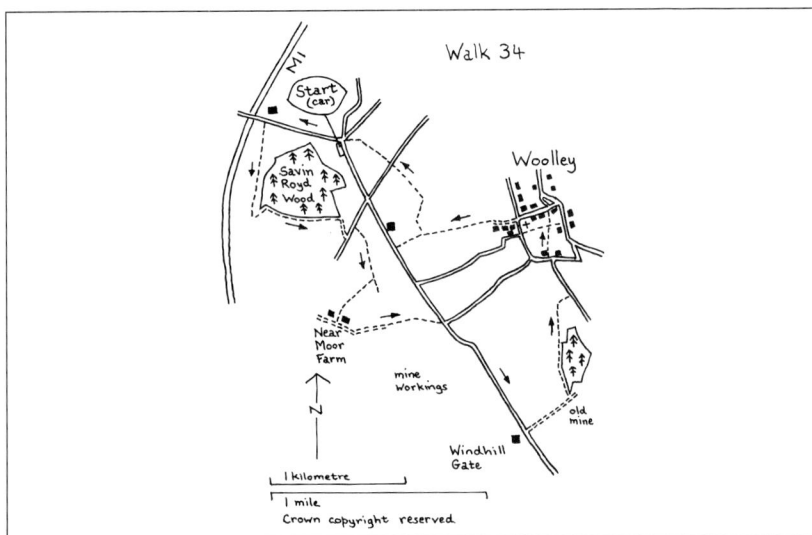

Walk 34

WOOLLEY
WALK 34

5 miles (8 km); Pathfinder 703. Woolley is a delightful village, and there are extensive views both west and east from the ridge of Woolley Edge.

By bus: _443/446 Leeds-Wakefield-Barnsley to Woolley village green. Walk along the High Street and start the walk at [*]._

By car: _There is a large layby on the road along Woolley Edge near the crossroads 250 yards north of Beacon Hill (GR 305 136). Park here._

From the crossroads walk downhill towards the M1. Just before the motorway bridge turn left along the signposted Walkway and follow the track into the wood with a field to the right. You are walking on top of a railway tunnel, hence the airshafts you pass, and many of the unevennesses in the terrain must be old spoil heaps from the tunnel. The track narrows to an elevated path, but you soon go down some steps on the right, then left down some more. Follow the clear path through the wood. Eventually the path bears left down some more steps and emerges into a field. Bear left along the bottom edge of the field, and when you reach the boundary wall of Savin Royd Wood, turn right and walk up the edge of the field with the wood on your left.

Cross a stile and continue up beside the wood. At the top edge of the wood cross the stile and turn right along the track to the road. Turn left up the road for 100 yards to a signposted footpath on the right. Cross the stile and walk along the top edge of the field to the next stile. Walk up the enclosed path only for 3 yards, then turn right through a gap in the wall into the wood. Bear slightly right along a path which soon emerges from the bottom of the wood. Bear slightly right again to a marker post, turn left round it and head diagonally down the field, with a campsite up to your left, to a gap in the hedge. Go through and walk straight down the middle of the next field to the stile in the fence/wall, then carry on down the next field to the next stile. Now keep forward with a hedge to your right to enter the yard of Near Moor Farm through a gateway. Walk forward down the track, then turn left along a cross track. This rather distinguished old farm is derelict at the time of writing.

The track soon bears left and starts to climb, ending at a field. Continue up the right hand edge of the field, with mine workings over the hedge/fence, and near the top enter the remains of an old hedged way, which soon narrows to a fenced path which turns sharp right, then sharp left and ends. A clear path leads up through the wood to Woolley Edge Lane. Immediately opposite is the memorial to several victims of an accident in June 1993. Ignore Gipsy Lane, signposted to Woolley, and turn right along the road, which is busy, but the verge can normally be used. It is a kilometre to Windhill Gate, the first large farm on the right, and opposite it on the left (just before a sign saying Welcome to Barnsley) a track leaves the road. Follow this old mine access road, but where it enters a wood turn left off it over a stile and follow the outside edge of Wheatley Wood.

At the far end of the wood cross the stile in the fence on the right and keep the line you have just been following along the edge of the wood over the next huge field. There is a very extensive view right. Soon Woolley Hall College comes into view, followed by Woolley village further left, and as you come over the brow of the hill you will see that you are coming closer to a fence on the right. Make for a gate in it, cross the stile nearby and walk down the edge of the next field with the hedge on your left. Turn left along the road, and at the next junction turn left (Back Lane) for about 60 yards, then turn right down a track to the right of a house, and where this turns left cross the stile in the wall on the right (by the name South Cottage) and walk straight over the large field. Ahead of you a line of trees, an old path to the church, crosses the field. Aim to pass between the third and fourth of these trees from the right, and you will reach a stile in the far right hand corner of the field. It leads into an enclosed path which you follow to the road in the attractive village of Woolley.

Turn left [*] along the High Street, but where this turns left and becomes Church Street, with Finkle Street to the right, keep forward along the no through road. The lane soon leaves the village and becomes an unsurfaced track, which ends at a large gate. Go through the small gate beside this and continue with the hedge to your left. In the next field corner ignore the stile ahead and turn right with a fence on your left. Again there are extensive views to the right. In the far corner of the field go through the wide gateway, bear slightly left and keep following the fence on your left. Go through the next facing gate and keep forward, now with an old wall on your left. The next gate leads out onto a road.

Cross this and go through the gate opposite. Walk along the right hand edge of the field, through another gate, and on with the hedge on your right to the next gate into a small wood. Keep along the right hand edge of this, and where it ends, keep following the fence on your right, but when you draw near the far corner of the field, bear half left to cut the corner and walk along with an old wall/fence on your right to a gate into the wood. Walk straight down through the wood to the next road. Turn left along it to return to the starting point of the walk. Walkers who came by bus will now jump to the start of the walk description.

YORKSHIRE SCULPTURE PARK AND BRETTON COUNTRY PARK
WALK 35

5 miles (8¼ km); Pathfinder 703. A fascinating outdoor exhibition of sculpture, a country park, tracks and field paths. Both the Sculpture Park and the Country Park have Information Centres and toilets, and there is a café in the Sculpture Park. Because the exhibitions of sculpture change frequently, it is not possible to describe a route round them: the Park needs to be explored at leisure. I merely suggest a possible route through it. Part of the walk spills over into the Barnsley and Kirklees Districts.

By bus: No.484 Leeds-Wakefield-Holmfirth to West Bretton, then walk down the Bretton Hall access road to the Sculpture Park Information Centre and start the walk at [*].

By car: Leave the M1 at Junction 38 and follow the A637 in the direction of Huddersfield; the entrance into Bretton Country Park is signposted a short distance along on the left (pay and display car park and Visitor Centre).

Leave the car park by the motorists' exit on the right, passing through the gates by the lodge, and turn right along the main road by the footway, which soon joins a bit of old road. Follow this to its end, then keep forward again on a footway. Pass the bus stop and a layby (which may have a van serving hot and cold snacks) (and enter Barnsley District) and turn right down Jebb Lane into Haigh. Shortly after the road bends left take a signposted track on the right (you are following the Country Park's Blue Trail). At the end of the track go through the gate into the field and follow the track forward. It bears left at the corner of the wood and runs parallel to the wood towards a fence. Cross the stile by the gate in the fence and turn right round the edge of the field, turning left with it when you reach the wood.

At the top of the wood cross the stile in the fence on the right and immediately go left to cross another stile, then keep forward, now following the Red Trail. The path is never in doubt, but red-topped marker posts provide reassurance that you are on the right line. There is a fine view over the lake to the Hall. Pass to the right of a small pond and old hedge, ignoring the track curving right, and continue across the middle of the next field to a stile. Keep your line over the next field, passing to the right of an enormous wooden bench, to reach a cross track and a stile. Here you leave the Red Trail, which turns right down the track. Cross the stile and keep roughly your line over the next field, heading for a small wood to the left of the large conifer plantation. The path bears left to a stile at the left hand corner of this wood. Cross (here you enter Kirklees District) and walk down the right hand edge of the next field to a stile onto a road just to the left of a farm.

Turn left along the road for 35 yards to a stile on the right and walk straight down the middle of the next field. Cross the stile and footbridge

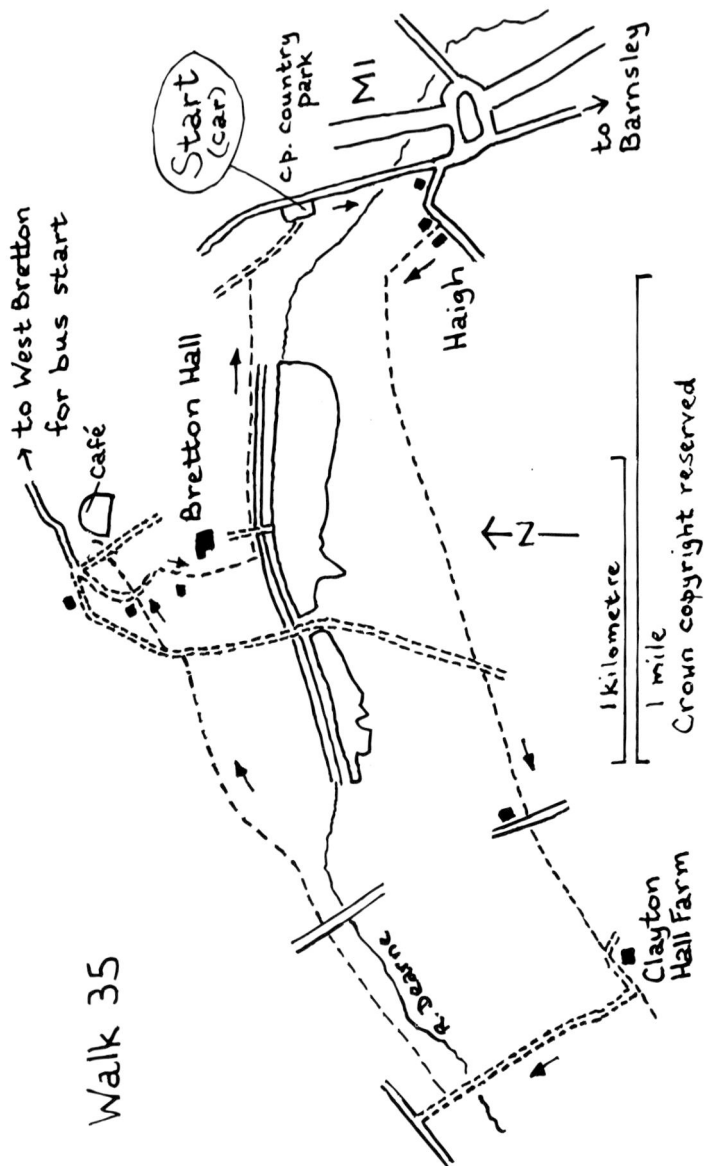

Walk 35

Start (car)

c.p. country park

M1

to Barnsley

Haigh

to West Bretton
for bus start

café

Bretton Hall

←N—

1 kilometre
1 mile
Crown copyright reserved

R. Dearne

Clayton Hall Farm

and follow the fence up to Clayton Hall Farm. The tower of High Hoyland Church is visible on the left above the woods on Hoyland Bank. Pass to the right of the farm and keep forward along the access road, which soon bends right downhill. Clayton West is over to the left. Pass Clayton West Waste Water Treatment Works and cross the River Dearne, and in 100 yards cross the stile on the right (here joining the Dearne Way) and walk straight across the middle of the large field. Cross the stile by a large solitary ash tree where the hedge becomes a wooden fence and bear right to the next stile. The River Dearne is close by on the right. Walk across the next large field to the stile already visible in the wall on the far side about 50 yards to the left of the stone bridge.

Cross the road to the stile opposite and follow the clear path through the wood to the next stile into a field. Walk along its left hand edge, and when the fence turns sharp left go half left to cross a wooden footbridge over Bentley Brook and re-enter the Wakefield District. Bear half left up the slope to a stile in the top corner, then cross straight over the next field to the next stile. Now follow the fence on your left until you reach a cross track and turn left along it, in a few yards keeping right at the fork into the Sculpture Park. The totem pole over the fence on the right is part of the award-winning Access Sculpture Trail, laid out mainly between 1985 and 1990, for which a detailed guide is available in the Information Centre. There is an entrance into it a short distance further along. Keep forward along the left hand edge of the car park and bear left to reach the Information Centre. There are toilets in the building on the left.

[*] To visit the Pavilion Gallery, the Bothy Shop and Gallery and the Bothy Café, with the Information Centre on your left cross the access road and walk up the grass opposite, towards a white roof visible beyond a hedge. Pass some Barbara Hepworth sculptures, cross another access road, walk up the broad steps and turn left along the tall hedge to find a gap in it at the end. Return by the same route to the Information Centre, and leaving it on your right, enter the car park and bear left through it. Turn right in front of the modern college building. Now the old tennis courts and the attractive Camellia House (by Wyatville, c.1817) are ahead of you.

Walk round the Camellia House by the left to the other side, then down the broad steps, bearing very slightly right at the bottom over the grass. Cross over a cross track and continue forward to the canal, turning left along its bank and passing below Bretton Hall. Cross another tarmac drive (with a bridge to the right) and keep forward to pass along a short section of path between trees and through a gate into Bretton Country Park. Keep forward with the canal to your right. Canada geese have left many unpleasant traces of their presence along here. When you draw level with a charming 18th-century bridge, bear half left over the grass, passing well to the right of the wood, to a marker post, then on to a cross track. Turn right along it. Fork left off it to reach the Country Park car park, Information Centre and toilets through gates. (Those who came by bus will now turn to the start of the walk description.)

NETHERTON, BULLCLIFF WOOD AND HORBURY CUT

WALK 36

8 miles (13 km); Pathfinder 703. Farmland, woodland and canal, with distant views and (for car walkers!) a pub halfway round.

By bus: 264 Wakefield-Huddersfield, 265 Wakefield-Netherton, 260/261 Dewsbury-Huddersfield, 216 Leeds-Overton to Church Lane, Netherton. Walk along Church Lane, passing to the right of the church, and turn right at the T-junction for about 100 yards, turn right up High Ridge and start the walk description at [#] below.

By car: On the A636 Wakefield-Denby Dale road, 300 yards on the Denby Dale side of the roundabout at the junction with the A637 on Bretton Common, opposite a minor road on the right there is a car park on the left. Park here. If it is full, there are laybys along the minor road.

Cross the stile by the gate at the back of the car park and follow the track. At the first crossing of tracks turn left. Wilderness Plantation is to your left. A stile by a gate leads out on to the A637. Cross over and turn left for a few yards, past a large water tank, then take the signposted footpath on the right and walk along the edge of the wood with a wall to your right. Soon a fine view opens up to Wakefield and beyond. After a time the path bears left away from the wall and you leave the wood by a stile. Turn right along the fenced path, and where it ends keep following the new fence on your right, which soon turns left and leads down to the A636.

Cross the road and turn right along the footway. Immediately after an old colliery entrance, now blocked, a footpath sign points left. Walk forward up the old road, soon passing between fences and through a gateway. Follow the track until it reaches another gateway into a field (on the left is a telegraph pole, nearby on the right a power line pole). Pass through a gap in the fence on the right and find a path which keeps as close as possible to the left hand edge of the wood (not clear at the start, but unproblematical after a short distance). The path leads to a ladder-stile. Over this keep forward near the edge of the wood, soon picking up a stone wall, which you keep on your right. Bullcliff Farm is over to the left. Cross a wooden stile in the wall and follow the path through Bullcliff Wood to a tarmac road. Cross over to the continuation of the footpath opposite. When you reach a cross track turn left along it,

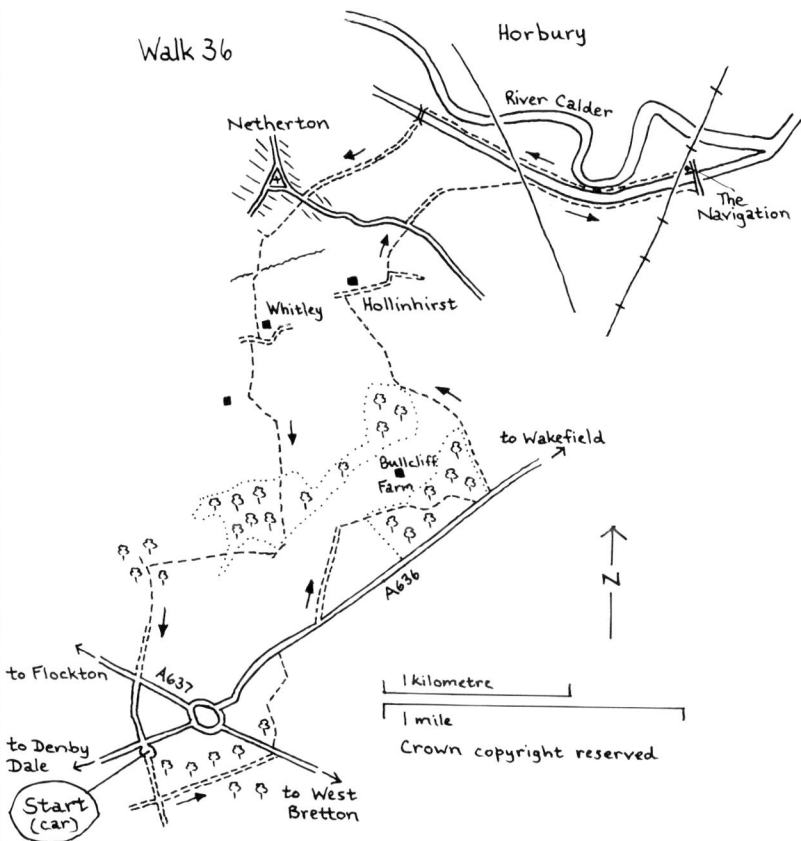

Walk 36

Horbury

River Calder

Netherton

The Navigation

Whitley

Hollinhirst

to Wakefield

Bullcliff Farm

A636

N

to Flockton

A637

to Denby Dale

Start (car)

to West Bretton

1 kilometre

1 mile

Crown copyright reserved

but where this broad ride bears left, a marker post points you right off it along another ride, which leads back to the A636.

Turn left along the footway as far as the end of the wood on the left, then turn left and follow the outside edge of the wood. Just after the far end of the wood cross the stile ahead and walk straight over the next field. Cross a small footbridge and climb a few steps at the next old field boundary, then keep forward over the next large field towards the wood. Pass a tall footpath sign and cross the stile in the bottom corner of the field. Keep the same direction through the narrow wood, cross the footbridge and climb some steps out of the wood. Turn left along the bottom edge of the field, but soon you turn right and follow the hedge on your left up to a stile, then walk half left over the next field to a stile by a gate. Cross this and the next one by another gate on the left, then turn right up the field edge towards Hollinhirst Farm. Bear left as you approach the top of the field, to a stile to the left of a holly bush.

Turn right along the track through the farmyard and out the other side. At the end of a section of wall on the left cross the stile on the left and walk along the left hand edge of the field. The Calder valley and Horbury come into view. Follow the fence round until you reach a stile in it, cross this and bear half right down the next field to a stile onto the road. Cross with care and take the track opposite. This narrows to an attractive woodland footpath and leads down to the canal (Calder and Hebble Navigation). Keep forward parallel to the canal. Cross a stile into a field, and now you are down to canal level. Pass a lock, cross a stile, go through a tunnel under the railway bridge, and just before the next bridge over the canal bear right then left and cross the bridge.

The Navigation pub is in front of you, for car drivers the halfway point of the walk and a welcome refreshment stop. Turn left through the car park to reach the canal towpath and turn right along it. Follow it to the next bridge, cross this and walk up the tarmac road, Balk Lane, to its junction with the motor road in Netherton. Cross the road and turn left for a yard or two, then [≠] right up High Ridge, keeping close to the fence on the right to enter a ginnel, which leads to a stile.

Cross straight over the yard to the stile opposite to the left of a large shed, then follow the right hand edge of the field, with playing-fields over the fence, until the fence turns sharp right. Here walk half left over the field to a stile in the fence opposite, then bear slightly left over the next field to the next stile, then follow the fence on the right along to the next stile. Drop down some steps, cross the beck by a bridge and climb the steps on the other side. Bear right across the yard to the stile opposite, then walk up the next field with a hedge to your left. There's a splendid view back and right to Wakefield.

Cross the stile in the top corner of the field, then the farm access road, and continue along the left hand edge of the next field with Whitley Farm to your left. Cross the stile in the next field corner and turn right along the track for 40 yards to a footpath sign pointing left. Cross the stile and walk down to the bottom left hand corner of the field, where there is another stile. Cross the footbridge and following stile and walk along the left hand edge of the next field. Cross the footbridge in the bottom left hand corner of the field, bear left, pass through a gap in the fence and walk down the edge of the field with a fence to your left.

Where the hedge on the left ends, to be followed by a stile, fork half right across the large field, following the line of a newly planted hedge to a new fence on the far side. Walk down with the fence on your right to find a gap in it at the bottom, go through and walk along for a few yards to a stile, then turn left and cross the beck by a stone bridge. Follow the path up into the wood. Climb the bank and turn right along the path, but after a few yards turn left off it, down the bank and on up through the wood. Cross straight over a track and follow the clear path up to a stile at the top edge of the wood. Turn right along the path between a fence and the wood, cross the stile at the end and keep forward for 30 yards, then turn right through a gap in the fence and walk down the next field, bearing left round the bottom of the slope and continuing along the field to a stile on the far side back into the wood (the post of the stile has a yellow top).

Bear left down through the wood, cross a sleeper bridge and leave the wood by another stile. Bear half left over the next field, cross a stile and another sleeper bridge and keep the same direction over the next large field to the stile in the fence on the far side. Cross the stile into the wood and walk forward, but turn left along a clear cross path. Cross to a stile in the fence at the left hand end of a wooden catwalk and bear left on the clear path up through the wood, very soon crossing another stile.

Walk forward to a grassy area, ignore the stile to the right and cross over to pass a large holly tree and continue on a clear path, soon meeting an old stone wall which you keep on your left. Ignore a stile on the right, cross a stile by a gate ahead, and when you reach a cross track, bear right along it. The track leads to the A637. To the right the Black Bull can be seen, and Emley Moor mast is prominent. Cross over and follow the minor road opposite, then cross the next main road into the car park. Bus walkers will now turn to the start of the walk description.

BANK WOOD AND STONY CLIFFE WOOD
WALK 37

6½ miles if coming by bus, 5¾ for motorists (10¼ /9¼ km); Pathfinder 703. A most attractive mix of old tracks and woodland paths in undulating countryside with good views, two nature reserves and much of historical interest. Much more information can be found in the Wakefield Countryside Service leaflet *Three easy to follow walks around Middlestown and Midgley.*

By bus: *128/129 Wakefield-Dewsbury, 263 Wakefield-Huddersfield, to the White Swan, near the crossroads in Middlestown. Walk up Cross Road, but where it swings right and becomes Old Road, keep straight forward along Carr Lane, a No Through Road. In the bottom of the dip the road swings left. Ignore a bridleway forking right here (your return route) and join the walk description at [#] below.*

By car: *On the A636 Wakefield-Denby Dale road, 300 yards on the Denby Dale side of the roundabout at the junction with the A637 on Bretton Common, opposite a minor road on the right there is a car park on the left. Park here. If it is full, there are laybys along the minor road.*

Walk to the far end of the car park, cross the stile by the gate and take the track through the woods. Shortly after passing a viewing platform on the right turn right at a cross track and follow it down through the wood. Leave the wood by a gate and cross a track leading to Bower Hill Farm on the right. Keep down the tree-lined track to the A636, cross and take the Emley road opposite. Turn right along the access road to Bentley Grange, but before you do, look left to the grassy hillock which is the remains of bell pits, where monks of Byland Abbey who owned Bentley Grange used to mine iron. At the entrance into the farmyard go through the gap by the gate on the right and walk along the track to the right of the buildings, passing through another gate on the way. At the end of all the buildings bear right with the track and continue with a high hedge on your left.

On reaching a wide gap in the hedge bear half right down the field to a stile on the edge of the wood. Cross this and the footbridge beyond and walk along with Bank Wood Beck on your right until you reach stepping stones over it. Cross these and the stile ahead into Bank Wood and bear left up through it. The path soon bears left parallel to the beck down below, but look out for a sleeper bridge on the right followed by a flight of steps climbing through the wood. At the top cross over a grassy ride and in a few yards ignore a minor track forking right. You are on Furnace Hill, where charcoal was burnt and iron smelted in the 14th century.

On reaching the top of the hill turn left along a cross track, but after 80 yards fork right off it on a footpath up some more steps. Cross the stile out of the wood and keep forward to the right of a hedge. At Bank

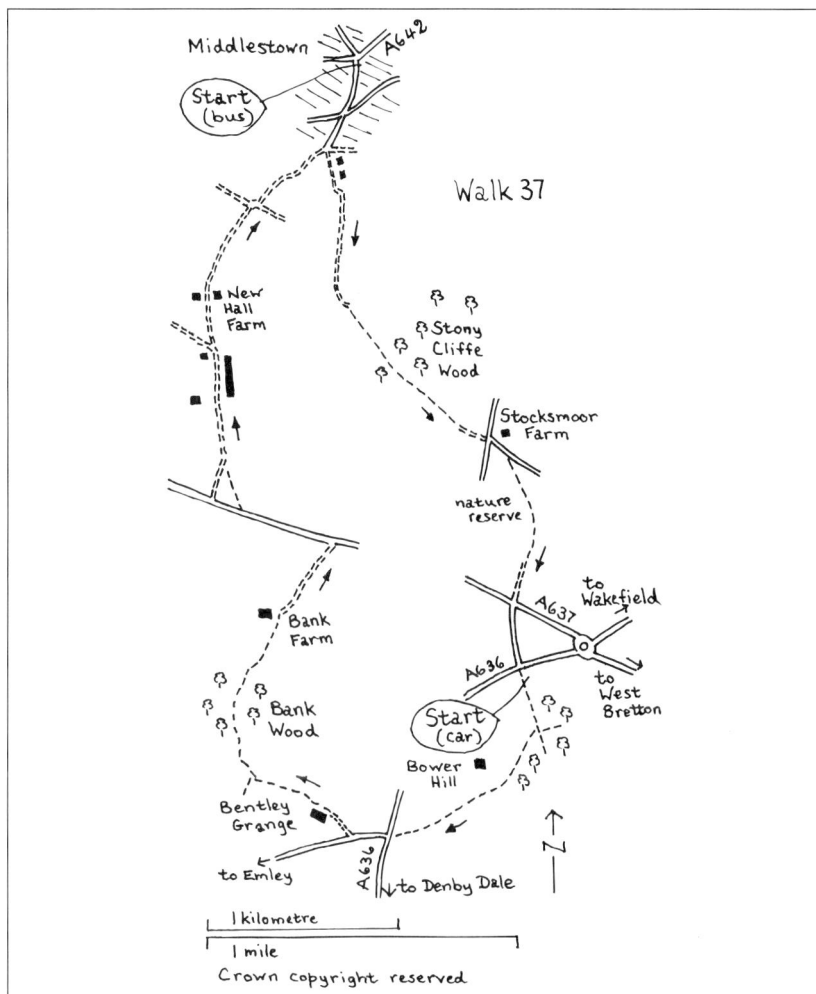

Walk 37

Crown copyright reserved

Farm go through a gate, walk along the right hand edge of the farmyard, and follow the access road up to the A637. Cross to the footway and turn left. Shortly before the water tower a footpath sign points right over a stile. Bear slightly left over the field to a stile in the bottom corner. Turn left through the gate then right down the tarmac access road to New Hall Detention Centre. Follow the road straight through between the houses, but where just after the telephone kiosk it turns left, keep straight on up a narrow lane.

Follow the track through New Hall Farm, noticing the remains of the mediaeval moat and the carved head on the building on the right which came from a 13th-century chapel which once stood near here. On reaching a junction of tracks keep straight on, in a few yards keeping left at the fork. This is Chapel Hill Lane, once the main road between Wakefield and Huddersfield. On reaching the first house in Middlestown, car walkers will turn right to continue the walk, bus walkers will turn left to return to the centre of Middlestown.

[#] Follow Carr Lane, which after a time drops, swings right and climbs again. Ignore a track forking off left on this slope. Carr Lane becomes a most attractive narrow hedged way, clearly of great age. Follow it all the way down to cross a footbridge and enter the nature reserve of Stony Cliffe Wood and continue on the broad rising track with a fence on the left. The path leads up through the wood, leaves it, and a short stretch of narrow hedged path leads to a tarmac road. Bear left up this, and at the crossroads go straight over and along the narrow road opposite. After 150 yards, having passed Stocksmoor Farm, fork right off the road by a notice which says Stocksmoor Common Nature Reserve.

Just before a stile the path forks. Cross the stile and follow the path through the wood, pass a redundant stile and walk along a section of boardwalk. At the end of this ignore the stile on the right and keep forward. Ignore another stile in a fence ahead and bear left, then right, to follow the boundary wall of the reserve on your left. Cross a stile by a gate and in 20 yards bear right along a track which leads to the A637. Cross over and follow the minor road opposite. Cross the A636 to reach the car park. Bus walkers should now go to the start of the walk description to continue the walk.

The Country Code

Enjoy the countryside and respect its life and work.

Guard against all risk of fire

Leave all gates as you find them: closed, if they are closed, open, if they are open.

Keep your dogs under close control.

Keep to public paths across farmland.

Use gates and stiles to cross fences, hedges and walls.

Leave livestock, crops and machinery alone.

Take your litter home.

Do not pollute any water.

Protect wildlife, plants and trees.

Take special care on country roads.

Make no unnecessary noise.

THE COXLEY VALLEY AND EMROYD COMMON
WALK 38

5½ or 6 miles (8¾ or 9½ km); Pathfinder 703. Old paths and tracks and superb views. The countryside between Middlestown and Netherton is so attractive that I have included alternative walks: the longer has more woodland paths, but both use historic routes through undulating country and have good views.

By bus: 264 Wakefield-Huddersfield, 265 Wakefield-Netherton, 260/261 Dewsbury-Huddersfield, 216 Leeds-Overton to Church Lane, Netherton.

By car: Park in Church Lane, Netherton.

Cross Netherton Lane and go down Bridle Lane opposite. When the road turns right as Bridle Close keep forward down the hedged and paved footpath, which has excellent views. On the edge of the Coxley Valley the path turns left (ignore a path right here) and drops into the valley. At a cross track turn right, cross the turning area and walk up through Coxley. Just after a field on the left and a large metal gate turn left along the signposted footpath between fences. Cross two stiles and keep forward along the left hand edge of the next field. Cross the stile in the top corner and walk half right over the next field to a stile onto an access drive. This stile is just to the right of a gate across the drive. Cross the drive and walk up the next field to the right of the hedge.

Cross the road and turn left up the footway. At the top of the hill just before the houses begin on the right turn right along the signposted footpath, which leads to Middlestown crossroads. Cross the A642 at the traffic lights and bear right along the front of the Little Bull and along a tarmac lane. Again the views are extensive. When the surface ends keep forward along the path. Ignore a hedged track on the right. Cross a stile, walk along the left hand edge of a paddock, cross another stile and turn left along an enclosed footpath. Cross straight over the next road (there is a nice view to Thornhill Edge) and follow the way between hedges, soon entering the wooded Emroyd Common. Here there are many paths you can explore, but our walk keeps to the main one, after a time passing to the left of a small pond. Shortly after this, when the main track swings left, keep forward along a narrower path which soon reaches the far side of the wood at a stile. Walk straight over the field to the next stile in the hedge opposite. There is another nice view of Thornhill Edge. Keep the same line over two more fields and through a small wood to reach a stile out onto a track at a junction. Take the fenced track straight ahead, which drops towards the valley of Smithy Brook.

You reach the next junction at Mug Mill Farm. Turning right here would take you over Smithy Brook and up to Thornhill Edge, but we turn left up Briggs Lane, a hedged way of some antiquity to judge by the

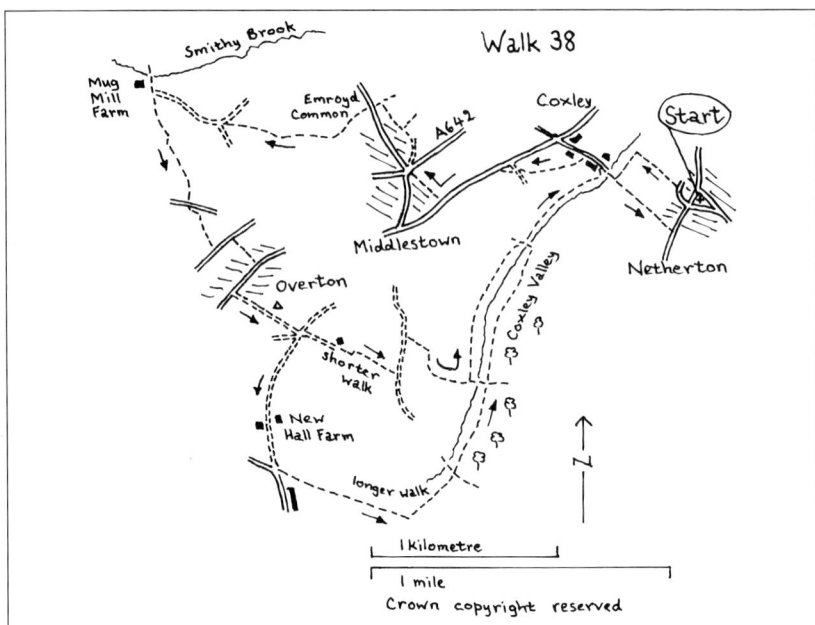

Walk 38

Smithy Brook

Mug Mill Farm

Emroyd Common

A642

Coxley

Start

Middlestown

Overton

Coxley Valley

Netherton

Shorter walk

New Hall Farm

longer walk

N↑

1 Kilometre

1 mile

Crown copyright reserved

causey stones which soon start. The hedged path ends at a stile. Bear slightly right across the field to another stile and a road. There is a bench here. Cross straight over to the stile opposite. At the moment you turn sharp left to follow the left hand edge of the field along to a gate, then go through this and turn right, following the fence on your right to a stile near the far corner of the field, but the correct line of the right of way may soon be restored, which would mean that from the stile you keep straight forward over the field to cross a stile into the next field, and then cross the next stile in the corner of that field. Bear slightly left over the next field to a gate near the far fence. Go through a gap beside this gate and turn left up the track, soon bearing right up to a stile out onto New Road.

Turn left along the footway for 100 yards to a signposted track on the right. Walk up this, but cross a stile in the fence on the right and go half left to cut the corner of the field to another stile. Keep your line for a few more yards, then bear left along a path over this rough ground which leads to a stile out onto the road in Overton. Turn right and at the top of the hill turn left along Smithy Lane. The tarmac ends at the trig point, and you keep straight along the dirt track. At the next T-junction stop and have a look around. Over to the left are the Gawthorpe Water Tower and the spire of Ossett Parish Church. Coming further right, the Cathedral and County Hall in the centre of Wakefield are prominent and further right again on the horizon are the power stations at Ferrybridge and Eggborough. Over to the right is the Emley Moor television mast.

102

For the longer walk. Turn right at the T-junction along the track between hedges. Walk straight through New Hall Farm, once part of the Bretton Estate. On the left is an old dovecote dated 1759, and just after it over on the left are the remains of an old moat. Just as you reach the first buildings of New Hall Detention Centre take the track on the left, signposted as a footpath, on the line of an old railway which used to transport coal from Denby Grange mine to the Calder and Hebble Canal, and follow it until it bears slightly right through a large gate. Leave it here, and take the track straight ahead, soon forking left along a clear path into New Hall Wood.

Follow the main path down to cross a beck, then keep straight on, soon with a beck on your left. Essentially we are going to follow this beck all the way through the woods to Coxley. You cross a footbridge over a small side beck, and eventually another footbridge with a pond on the right, after which you have a fence to your right and in a few yards reach a cross track. Cross over and cross the stile straight ahead. Now keep always on the clear path nearest to the beck. At one point you will cross a side beck by a broad plank bridge, then you must ignore the stepping stones over the main beck, with steps climbing to a field. Follow the beck on your left until it flows into a lake, and cross it by the footbridge. Cross the stile on the right immediately after the footbridge.

For the shorter walk. Turn left at the T-junction, but immediately fork right. Having passed a house the lane narrows to a hedged path. Where this ends, turn left along the field edge and soon follow the edge as it turns right. On reaching a cross track, Carr Lane, turn left up it. When the track begins to drop, look out for another track forking off on the right with a hedge on its left, and follow that. The track turns sharp right and then sharp left again, still with a hedge on the left. When it curves left again, leave it and walk straight down the field, passing to the left of two trees. At the edge of the wood there is a footpath sign. Turn left with a fence and the wood on your right.

Keep along just outside the wood until you reach a grassy field on the right. Turn down right, still following the edge of the wood. Cross a stile and walk along the edge of the field with the Coxley Beck on your right. Cross another stile and walk along between a fence and the beck. Cross a stile and bear slightly left across the field to the next stile.

Now the longer and the shorter walks have joined up again. Walk along with the fence and lake on your right to the next stile, which leads back into the woods. Follow the fenced path forward, crossing more stiles on the way, until you have another lake to your right and a high breeze-block wall on the left. Follow this round to the left and turn right at a cross track to reach Coxley Lane. Turn right down it, cross over the turning area at the bottom and cross the stile by the large gate ahead. Follow the track up to Netherton. At the top follow the tarmac path on the left of the track to Netherton Lane and turn left to return to the starting point.

HORBURY BRIDGE TO CHICKENLEY
WALK 39

6½ miles (10¼ km); Pathfinder 692, 703. Field paths, disused railways, an attractive stretch of canal towpath and fine views of the Calder valley. The walk includes 3 km of the Kirklees Way.

By bus: 128/129 Wakefield-Dewsbury, 263/264 Wakefield-Huddersfield, 265 Wakefield-Middlestown, 216 Leeds-Middlestown, 278 Netherton-Ossett to Horbury Bridge.

By car: You may find room to park at Horbury Bridge on Bridge Road opposite the school, otherwise turn right in front of the Horse & Jockey and follow the minor road towards South Ossett. This climbs and swings left and on this bend there is a large layby on the right. Park here and start the walk at [#].

Between the river and canal bridges turn into the lane on the opposite side of the road to the Bingley Arms. When the surface ends keep on along the track, and just before this enters a field look right for a view of a delightful little marina, then go left onto the towpath of the Calder & Hebble Navigation and turn right along it. There follows an attractive stretch of peaceful rural canal. Pass two locks, a house and a small bridge over a cut on the right and immediately fork right (here joining the Kirklees Way) on a path which leads through a tunnel under the railway. Now you have the Calder close by on the right. Pass through another tunnel under railway lines and then under a substantial railway bridge and keep forward by the river, which you soon cross by a footbridge.

Walk on to reach a tarmac road and turn left along it, to pass through a gap-stile by a large metal gate and enter the grounds of a factory. Walk along the right hand edge of these, pass to the left of a modern bungalow and keep on up the lane with a high wall on your right. Ignore a track forking right to a stile by a large gate and keep on along the right hand edge of the factory yard, then the track outside the car park, to a stile by a double metal gate. Keep forward to find a narrow but clear footpath, which runs along the foot of the slope on the right, then just below the bottom edge of a field, with trees to the left, and soon with a wooden fence on the right.

When you are faced by the high metal fence of Dewsbury Sewage Works, pass to the right of it and bear right uphill with an old wall to your left. Just before the wall kinks left, cross through it and walk for a short distance with the remains of the wall on your right, then turn right again with the wall still on your right. When you reach a cross track, turn very sharply left down it. On the other side of the valley on the hill is Thornhill. In the bottom of the dip ignore a track coming in from the right, and as you climb again ignore another one forking left to Mitchell

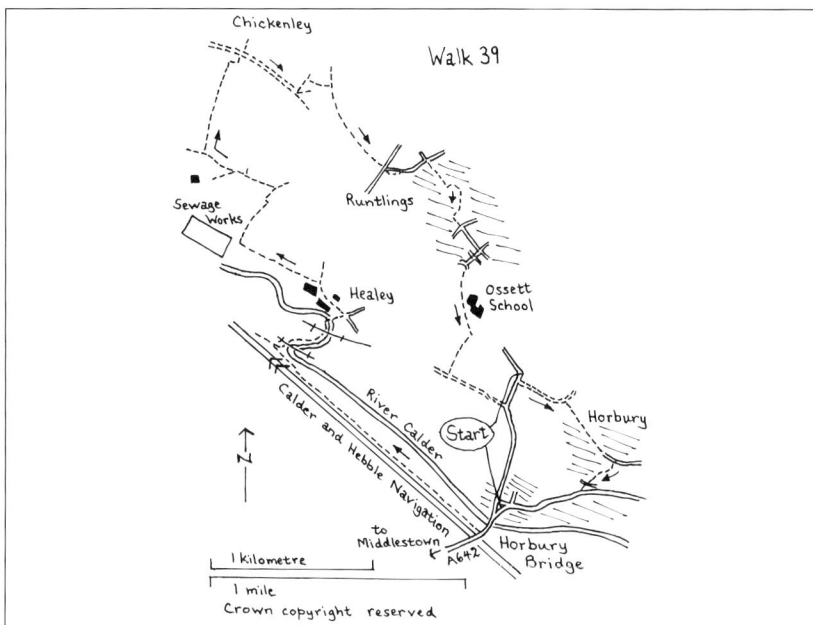

Walk 39

Chickenley
Sewage Works
Runtlings
Healey
Ossett School
Calder and Hebble Navigation
River Calder
Start
Horbury
to Middlestown
A642
Horbury Bridge

N

1 kilometre
1 mile
Crown copyright reserved

Laithes Farm. After crossing the brow of the hill follow the track as it turns sharp right, ignoring a footpath straight ahead, but where the track kinks left to cross a beck, leave it and keep straight on up the left hand edge of the field, with the beck and hedge down on your left. Keep the beck, which is also the boundary between Wakefield and Kirklees Districts, on your left until you are faced by a fence. Bear right, but when you reach a gap in the fence go through it and turn right along a broad track on the line of an old railway.

Follow the old railway line until it kinks left and splits into three: take the left hand path, keeping the small wood on your right, but shortly after the gradient eases fork right between metal posts onto a tarmac path and follow this across the park. There are fine views over the Calder valley. When you reach a tarmac cross path, turn right. When the tarmac ends, keep on along the grit path, eventually passing to the right of houses (ignore a path forking left up to them) until you reach the road in Runtlings through a kissing-gate. Cross the road, go through the barrier opposite and follow the path as it curves left to join a road. Bear right along this, noticing the old paving stones a cartwheel's width apart.

Now we wind our way through South Ossett, and close attention must be paid to route-finding! At the next junction turn right down the footway with a high hedge/fence on the left (ignoring the track on the right), pass the barrier and walk forward down Ash Close, turning left at the bottom to follow another tarmac path. At the T-junction turn right, but just before the entrance to Ossett Cricket Club turn left along an enclosed path. Follow it to the end, keep forward along the street and at the next junction keep forward along Dimple Wells Lane. Follow it to the very end and turn left along a ginnel. Cross the next road diagonally left to walk along Broomcroft Road opposite. Turn right down Valley View Road and at the T-junction at the bottom turn left along Healey Drive. After house no. 40 on the right go down the ginnel, which soon turns left and then right again. Now our tour of the houses is over!

At the end ignore a fenced path on the right and keep forward along the left hand edge of the field to pass Ossett School. Again there is a fine view up Calderdale. At the end of the field turn right with the fence downhill. There is a great array of railway sidings ahead. In the bottom of the second field, where the field edge curves right, go through the stile ahead and walk forward to another stile. Turn left along the track and follow it to the road. By turning right you could return quickly to Horbury Bridge, but there are more delights in store! So turn left uphill. Where the road curves left there is a large layby on the right (where you may have parked!).

[#] Take the signposted bridleway leaving the layby. Where the track bends left uphill, fork right off it along a tarmac path. Pass a metal barrier. This pleasant path leads through between gardens. At the end go down some steps on the right and turn left. The tarmac surface resumes and there is a fine Georgian house on the left. Look for a hedged ginnel on the right and follow it all the way down to a cross street. There is a fine 17th-century house on the left. Cross and climb the steps to the main road. Turn right to return to Horbury Bridge.

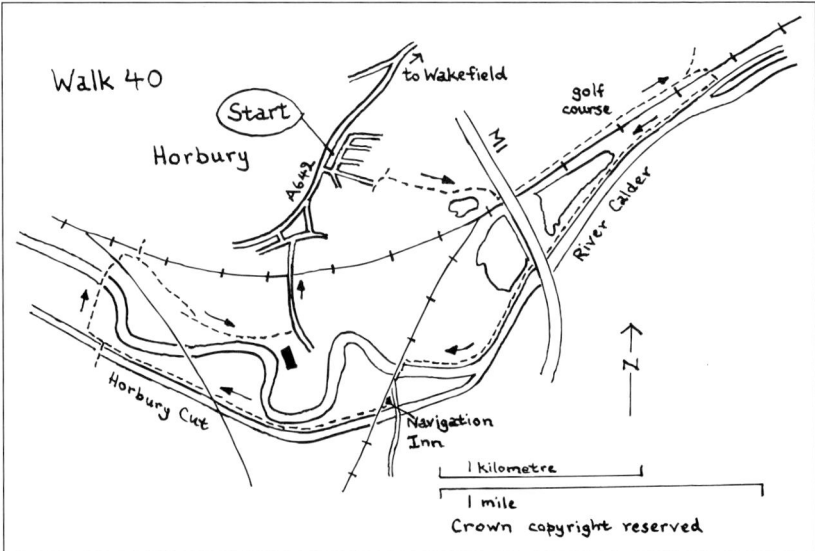

Walk 40

Horbury — Start — to Wakefield — golf course — M1 — River Calder — A642 — Horbury Cut — Navigation Inn — N↑ — 1 kilometre — 1 mile — Crown copyright reserved

HORBURY: CANAL AND RIVER
WALK 40

5½ miles (9 km); Pathfinder 703. Mainly canal and riverside walking.

By bus: _128/129 Wakefield-Dewsbury, 263/264 Wakefield-Huddersfield, 265 Wakefield-Netherton to Northfield Lane, Horbury, about 200 yards on the Wakefield side of Horbury First School, by the playing fields of Horbury School._

By car: _Street parking on Northfield Lane parallel to the main road (A642) opposite the playing fields of Horbury School._

Turn down Parker Road off Northfield Lane. At the bottom turn left along the track, but in 40 yards cross the stile on the right and keep to the right of the old hedge down the left hand edge of the playing fields. Cross the next stile ahead and keep forward - there is no clear path - towards the lake. Pass through the line of an old hedge and keep forward to the next old field boundary a short distance from the lake, then bear half left across what can be very wet ground to a wooden step-stile in a fence. From it bear slightly left to a wooden footbridge over a ditch, then keep straight forward to the next stile near the foot of the motorway embankment. Cross it and walk forward to the fence, then bear right along this to a stile onto a metalled road.

Turn left under the motorway, then ignore the track turning right under the railway and keep forward through the bollards along a tarmac track. The Municipal Golf Course is over to your left, the railway on your right. Shortly before you reach the corner of the housing estate pass round a large metal gate across the track and fork right down an unsurfaced track which leads through the tunnel under the railway. Climb the embankment straight ahead, then drop down the other side and turn right along the towpath.

Soon you reach Thornes Flood Lock at the end of this cut, and bear right to rejoin the track. Follow it along parallel to the River Calder, pass under the M1 and keep on along the path, in a few yards forking left along the narrower river bank path. Over to your right is the Horbury Sailing Club. After a time you are separated from the river by dense trees and bushes, but when these end bear left and continue along the river bank. When you reach the railway bridge, don't pass under it, but go round to the left of the arch to find steps up onto a wooden catwalk inside the bridge, which allows you to cross the river. Drop down the steps on the far side and bear left along the lane to the Navigation Inn (drinks, meals and children's playground).

Walk to the bottom of the pub car park and turn right along the towpath of Broad Cut. After almost a mile pass under a footbridge over the canal, with a redbrick villa over to the right, and 100 yards further on turn right off the towpath over a stile and follow the path to an old railway bridge over the River Calder. On the far side bear half right down off the embankment and keep forward along the path. Pass under an old railway bridge, ignore the path forking right and walk up a few steps and turn right on an ascending path with the railway to your left. When you reach the road, ignore the railway bridge on the left and go right for 3 yards, then left on an old fenced path which continues to climb.

At the top walk along with a tall hedge to the left and pleasant views to the right until you reach a tarmac access drive. Cross this and continue along the old fenced path opposite (it may be choked with nettles, in which case move into the field on the left). When you reach a floodlit football pitch the fenced path bears right to a stile into a field. Walk down the right hand edge of the field to the next stile, then bear left and follow the fence down to a track at the bottom, and turn left along it. The track leads to the river bank. As you approach a mill, the track leaves the river and passes to the left of the buildings: when you reach a tarmac road turn left. Just after passing The Shutt on the left, cross the major road and turn right, and at the next junction keep straight forward up The Sycamores, keeping left when the road forks. A ginnel leads back to the A642. Turn right to return to the start.

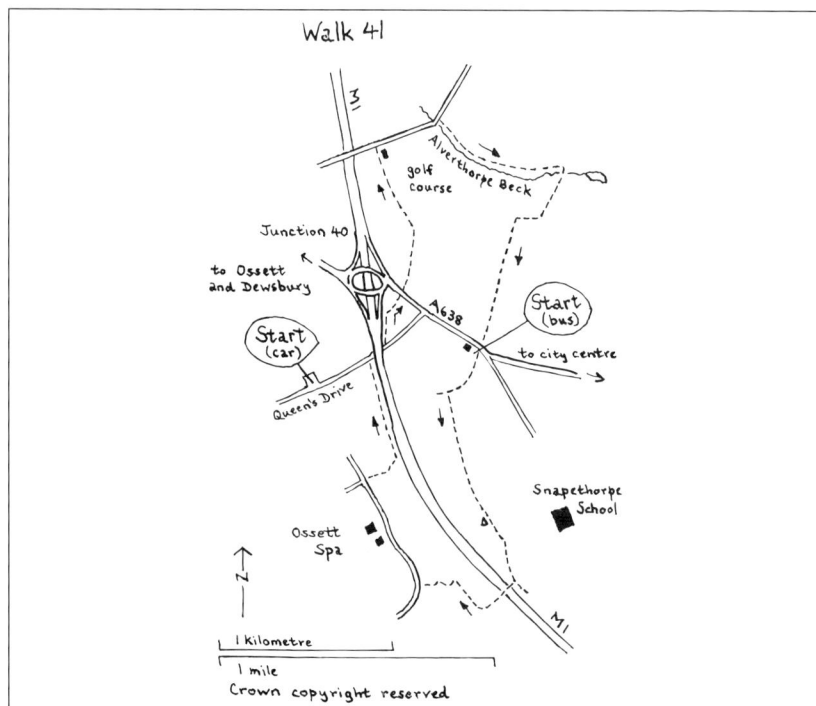

Walk 41

ALVERTHORPE BECK AND OSSETT SPA
WALK 41

5 miles (8 km); Pathfinder 692, 703. Beckside path, a golf course and some fine views.

By bus: 116/117/118 Wakefield-Leeds, 253/258/279 Wakefield-Dewsbury/Cleckheaton/Halifax, 269 Wakefield-Dewsbury/Cleckheaton to the Frog & Firkin (formerly the Malt Shovel) at the junction of Dewsbury Road and Broadway, Lupset.

By car: There is street parking near the Frog & Firkin, but I suggest you use the car park of Spring Mill Park on Queens Drive, 450 yards on the Ossett side of the underpass under the M1, walk back through the underpass and start the walk at [#].

Pass to the left of the Frog & Firkin and keep forward along the track, but immediately after it passes under the power lines take the gravel footpath forking left back under the power lines, with houses to the left and a view to the Emley mast to the right. Follow the ridge along, soon with a good view right to Horbury, and eventually ahead of you is the M1 stretching away into the distance over the Calder valley. Half left are the playing fields and buildings of Snapethorpe Middle School. You pass a trig point on the right of the track, close to a wooden power line pole: in the 19th century this was called Mount Sorrell.

The track leads down to a footbridge over the M1. On the far side bear right and then left round a high wall. Follow the wall/fence down to cross a beck by a footbridge. Turn sharp right along the bottom edge of the field. Cross a stile by a gate and keep forward. As you approach some redbrick houses you are faced by a wooden fence: bear left and follow this fence round to the terrace of houses and along the track to Spring End Road. Turn right. The road passes through an industrial estate and then Ossett Spa. It is hard to believe that in the 1880s there were two bath houses making use of the spring waters. Pass The Fleece, then just after the telephone box on the right and opposite Manor Road turn right down Baptist Lane, which soon becomes an unsurfaced track. Just before the tunnel under the M1 turn left and follow the fence on the right along to the field corner and into a fenced path which leads to Queens Drive. Cross the road. Motorists will turn left to return to their cars, others will turn right to pass under the motorway.

[#] About 20 yards beyond the motorway underpass cross the stile in the fence on the left and walk along parallel to the motorway with the fence/hedge to your left. Pass through a gateway and bear half right, to follow the hedge on your right up. Cross two stiles to reach the A638 and cross the dual carriageway to the signposted path opposite. Go down the steps and into a hedged way. There is a view right to Wakefield city centre and half-right the tower of Alverthorpe Church is prominent. When the hedge on the right ends, keep on by the hedge on the left, and in a few yards you are back in the hedged lane. On reaching a cross track, the line of an old railway, turn left for 3 yards to a stile by a gate into Low Laithes Golf Club. Follow the track forward over the golf course, looking out for flying golf balls, to another stile by a gate. Walk on between the car park and the clubhouse to the road and turn right.

Cross the bridge over Alverthorpe Beck and in 20 yards, opposite the entrance to Low Laithes Farm, turn right along a track. The track narrows to a footpath parallel to the beck and golf course. Keep by the beck until you are faced by a massive pylon. Go left if you would like a look at the old mill reservoir, but our route crosses the footbridge on the right and follows the path parallel to the power lines. A few yards before reaching a high fence you cross the disused railway line again. Turn right along the fence. The path soon curves left and leads back to the A638 opposite the Frog & Firkin. (Motorists should now go to the start of the walk description.)

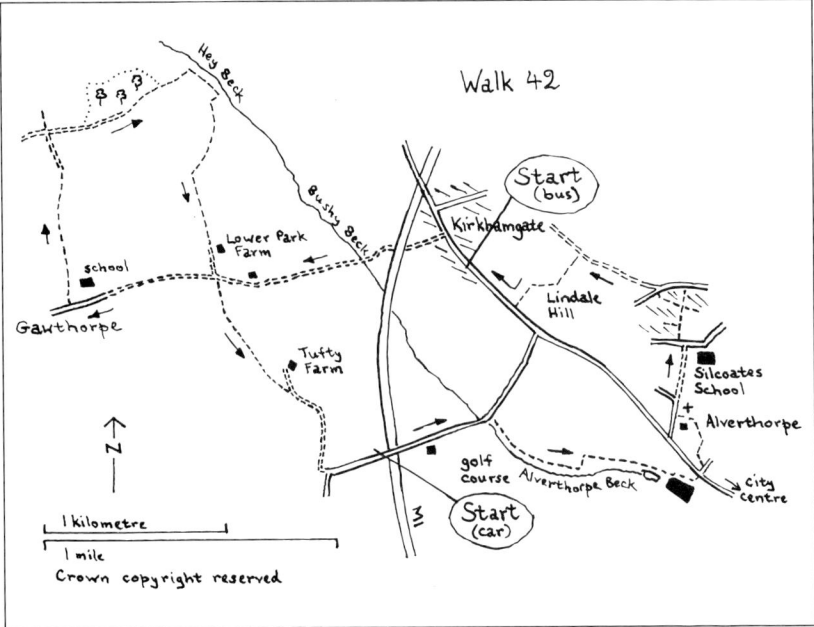

Walk 42

110

ALVERTHORPE, KIRKHAMGATE AND GAWTHORPE
WALK 42

7 miles (11¼ km); Pathfinder 692. Pleasantly rural field paths and tracks. The Wakefield skyline from the west.

By bus: No. *212 Wakefield-Dewsbury to the stop about 200 yards before Kirkhamgate post office.*

By car: *Just after the road from Low Laithes to Ossett crosses the M1 there is a layby with space for four or five cars. Park here and start the walk at [*] below.*

About 40 yards after passing Kirkhamgate post office, heading away from Wakefield, turn left down Gawthorpe Lane. Pass under the M1 by an underpass. The track bears left and descends gently to cross Bushey Beck Bridge. You reach a farm access track on a bend: bear left along it, keeping the farm on your right. After 220 yards ignore the next farm track on the right, and when the lane becomes tarmac, ignore another tarmac lane on the right. Keep forward to Gawthorpe, and leave North Ossett High School and its car park on your right. About 100 yards further on turn right along a signposted ginnel, tarmac at first.

When the tarmac ends keep to the left of the hedge ahead, along a fenced path. When the fenced section ends, cross a stile and keep forward along the right hand edge of the field. Cross the beck at the foot by a wooden bridge to the left of a concrete farm bridge, cross the stile and turn left up the fenced track. Your way now lies for a short distance in Kirklees District. When you reach a cross-track, turn right along it. It leads down to the right of Dogloitch Wood and ends at a gate into a field with a stile beside it. Continue down the left hand edge of the field to the bottom and bear right with the field edge, soon with Hey Beck on your left.

At the far end of the field follow the field boundary right again, but shortly cross the stile in the fence on the left leading to a footbridge and another stile (out of Kirklees and back into Wakefield!) and bear half right up the large field to the hedge at the top. Cross the stile in the top corner and follow the hedge on your right along to Lower Park Farm. Cross the stile by the gate and walk forward down the farm access road.

When you reach a cross track turn left for a few yards, then right at the footpath sign, and walk down the left hand edge of the next field. At the bottom the path crosses a footbridge and continues with a fence to the right. Cross a stile and keep on by the fence. When the fence turns right, bear half right to cross another footbridge, then left to the next stile, where a fence joins a hedge. Walk straight across the next field to the (redundant) stile on the far side, then follow the fence on your left. Shortly after passing the buildings of Tufty Farm down on your left, cross a stile in the fence and turn right along the access road. Follow this past Tufty Farm farmhouse and on to the next road, with a fine view to the Wakefield skyline. Bear left along the road.

[*] Walk across the motorway bridge, pass the entrance into Low Laithes Golf Club and follow the road as it crosses the bridge over Alverthorpe Beck. In 20 yards, opposite the entrance to Low Laithes Farm, turn right along a track. The track narrows to a footpath parallel to the beck and golf course. Keep by the beck until the wire fence you are following on your left turns sharp left away from the beck and the path forks. Go with the fence and after 20 yards turn right along a broad hedged way. Soon you are walking parallel to an old mill reservoir over on the right. The path passes to the left of the mill and then bears left round a grassy area beside the car park of the Blue Light pub to reach a street. Cross over this, pass the bollard and walk forward along the path ahead to reach Batley Road.

Cross straight over into Highfield Rise opposite, but in a few yards bear left into a works yard, at the far end of which is a modern bungalow. Walk through the yard to find at the left hand end of the bungalow wall a narrow footpath. Walk up this and at the top bear slightly left up the grass to the corner of the wall of Alverthorpe Church. Turn left along the clear cross path between the school grounds and the churchyard. At the road turn right, but when Childs Road curves left, keep forward along St.Paul's Drive. Pass to the left of the new estate of Silcoates Court, through the bollards and along the hedged path. After passing an entrance into Silcoates School on the right, the lane acquires a tarmac surface. On reaching the next road, turn left along the footway for 60 yards, then cross the road, pass through a barrier and walk along a paved footpath.

When the tall fence on the left turns left, ignore the path which follows it and keep forward, but when a paved path comes in from the right, turn left and walk along the left hand side of a grassy area. On reaching the next road, turn right, and cross straight over the next road to take Lindale Lane opposite. When the tarmac ends, keep forward along the track, pass to the right of an enormous pylon, and immediately after passing a fenced area full of old cars, fork left off the track, pass a barrier and climb the stepped path up Lindale Hill.

When you near the top take the clear path forking right, which leads to the grassy area on the summit. This is a reasonable viewpoint, although the view towards Wakefield is spoilt by power lines. The path descends past a wooden pylon and joins a track, which should be followed down to the Batley Road. Turn right to Kirkhamgate. Car walkers should now turn to the start of the walk description.